PENGUIN  CLASSICS

THE LIFE OF THE BUDDHA

TENZIN CHÖGYEL (1701–1767) was a prominent Bhutanese intellectual in the eighteenth century. He was an ordained monk and a prominent leader in the Drukpa Kagyu school of Buddhism. As the tenth Lord Abbot of Bhutan, he served as the state's highest ecclesiastical authority. A prolific author, he composed an influential history of Bhutan, *The Religious History of the South*; a biography of his teacher Tenzin Döndrup; several works of narrative literature; an abundance of exquisite liturgical verse; and, most famously, *The Life of the Lord Victor Shakyamuni, Ornament of One Thousand Lamps for the Fortunate Eon,* better known as *The Life of the Buddha* (completed in 1740).

KURTIS R. SCHAEFFER is an avid translator of classical Tibetan literature and a lifelong student of Tibetan and Himalayan Buddhist culture. He is the author or editor of nine books, including *Himalayan Hermitess, The Culture of the Book in Tibet,* and *Sources of Tibetan Tradition* (with Matthew T. Kapstein and Gray Tuttle). He lives with his family in Charlottesville, Virginia, where he teaches in the Department of Religious Studies at the University of Virginia.

TENZIN CHÖGYEL

The Life of
the Buddha

Translated with an Introduction and Notes by
KURTIS R. SCHAEFFER

PENGUIN BOOKS

PENGUIN BOOKS

Published by the Penguin Group
Penguin Group (USA) LLC
375 Hudson Street
New York, New York 10014

USA | Canada | UK | Ireland | Australia | New Zealand | India | South Africa | China
penguin.com
A Penguin Random House Company

This translation first published in Penguin Books 2015

ISBN 978-0-14-310720-0

Printed in the United States of America
1 3 5 7 9 10 8 6 4 2

Set in Sabon LT Std

Contents

Introduction

The Story of the Buddha:
A Narrative for Human Development

The Buddha was a human being. He struggled, he succeeded, he failed. He made difficult choices. He made mistakes of the sort we all might make. And he persevered. He lived in childlike innocence until he witnessed the unyielding reality of human suffering—poverty, sickness, old age, and death. He struggled with the implications of this suffering for his life and the lives of others. He had a family. He left his family. He worked as a teacher, a leader, and a community builder. He worried about his legacy. He grew ill as an old man and died.

The Buddha was a prince, the foremost younger member of a royal family and heir to the king's throne. He lived in utter luxury, wanting nothing. He received the finest education possible. He was a master of the arts, literature, athletics, and politics. He had many wives and lovers, and bore a son. He was to be a king, a god on earth. And then he cast the sweet life away when he realized that in spite of his exalted status he would still become ill, grow old, and die.

The Buddha was a reincarnation, the rebirth of a person now dead. He was a series of human beings, reborn through countless lifetimes. He had many bodies, many incarnations, though he remained in some sense himself, a "he," an individual, indivisible yet multiple. And as a reincarnation he is no different, according to Buddhist doctrine, from any other living being, save that he eventually came to understand the fundamental role of ethical cause and effect—the engine of rebirth—in creating his many rebirths, his many experiences in this life and all that had come before it. Because he came to understand rebirth as yet another form of human suffering, he sought, and found, an end to rebirth.

The Buddha was a god. He lived in celestial realms, in castles in the sky where gods enjoyed the divine fruits of their good acts over many eons. Yet the Buddha knew that even a god suffers from ethical cause and effect, that gods must descend from their celestial palaces if they wish to find an end to suffering, just like every other living being. He taught the gods the means to liberate themselves from the suffering that even they, as exalted celestial beings, experience. He was a god among gods.

The Buddha is a bodhisattva, a living, thinking being whose only goal is to achieve enlightenment—to fundamentally transform his understanding of reality—in order to truly put an end to human suffering. The Buddha is a savior, a being whose empathy for the suffering of others is so profound that he cannot but act on their behalf.

The Buddha was, is—ever will be—the cosmos. His "body" is coextensive with all that is. He is reality. As such he seeks, through the drama of human embodiment, to relieve the suffering that comes to those living beings who do not understand that they are this reality as well.

According to Buddhist traditions throughout Asia, the Buddha holds each and all of these identities within his capacious form. Stories of the Buddha from ancient, medieval, and modern traditions contain this multiplicity, at times emphasizing one aspect of his identity, at times

another, yet always deep with potential meaning, over-
flowing with possibilities for readers from all walks of
life. This is one such story.

The life story of Shakyamuni Buddha, the founder of
Buddhism who lived two and a half thousand years ago,
is perhaps the most important narrative in the Tibetan
Buddhist tradition. While the great Tibetan, Bhutanese,
and Mongolian masters of the past have had a more direct
impact on the course and contours of Buddhism in
Tibetan-speaking and Tibetan-reading lands, the story of
the founder, Shakyamuni, defines the very shape and
scope of Buddhism. A definition of suffering—the basic
human problem—an analysis of the causes of suffering,
an affirmation that human suffering can be alleviated,
and a demonstration of the steps needed to escape suffering are integrated within the life story of a single human
being, the Buddha. His story forms the blueprint for a life
dedicated to the two fundamental challenges faced by
people, the easing of suffering for oneself and for others.
And if this most basic goal is integral to the Buddha's
story, then any Buddhist leader in Tibet, Bhutan, or any-
where else in the world must emulate this story, must follow in the Buddha's footsteps, must live the life of a
Buddha, "the Enlightened One."

In Buddhist traditions of Tibet and the Himalayas this
blueprint for an ideal Buddhist life was formally expressed
in twelve major life episodes, "the twelve acts of the
Buddha."

The idea that the narrative of the Buddha's enlightenment could be reduced to a set of key episodes dates back
to at least the fifth century CE, when the *Analysis of the
Buddha Jewel*—a formative work for Indian and Tibetan
notions that all living beings possess the ability to achieve
enlightenment—outlined in a single verse Shakyamuni's

career in twelve acts, though without any further elaboration. Indian Buddhist literature never utilized this concise narrative structure to develop a full account of the Buddha, from birth to death. The most elaborate classical life of the Buddha, the *Living Out of the Game Scripture,* ends with the Buddha's teaching career. It does not include his death, the central event that was the catalyst for the spread of Buddhism, the cause of much philosophizing over the centuries, and the conundrum that the living ubiquitously face. This is not to say that there are no narratives of the Buddha's death in Indian Buddhist literature. The *Scripture of the Great Passing from Suffering,* dedicated in its entirety to the last days of Shakyamuni, is one of the most beautiful works of the Buddhist canonical literature from South Asia. Yet it was left to later writers in different cultures, writing in different languages, to craft synthetic portraits of the Buddha's life from time immemorial through birth to death. Tibetan writers, however, capitalized on the twelve-act structure, and the story before you now is one of the best examples of the genre. The structure is simple, and outlines the basic chronology of the Buddha's life:

1. Life in heaven (prebirth)
2. Descent to earth (conception and gestation)
3. Birth (age 1)
4. Education (ages 1 to 16)
5. The pleasures of his royal harem (ages 16 to 29)
6. Renunciation of house (age 29)
7. Spiritual discipline (ages 29 to 35)
8. Journey to Bodhgaya (age 35)
9. Battle with demons (age 35)
10. Enlightenment (age 35)
11. Teaching (ages 35 to 80)
12. Death (age 80)

The power of this biographical framework lies in the flexibility it allows individual authors: As long as these twelve major acts are treated, a writer is free to include more or less detail depending on one's intentions, be they primarily literary, didactic, historical, polemic, or otherwise. The author of the present biography, Tenzin Chögyel, uses this freedom to great effect. The jé khenpo, or chief abbot, of Bhutan, Tenzin Chögyel wrote this work during the golden age of Bhutanese literature, when biography was a major literary form. In his telling of the Buddha's life he endeavors at all times to tell a concise and quickly moving story that is at once exciting and emotionally engrossing. Occasionally he will stop to note an alternate version of a particular episode, or pause to speak directly to the reader about the proper way to pay reverence to the Buddha or to keep him in mind on holy days. Yet he never tarries long. Tenzin Chögyel is not interested in systematically laying out Buddhist doctrine or prescribing practice. His task is to tell a good story.

The story may be quickly summarized. The Buddha, whom Tenzin Chögyel refers to as the Bodhisattva before his enlightenment in chapter 10, spends his penultimate life in the celestial realm of Tushita, where he teaches the gods and appoints a successor, the future Buddha Maitreya (chapter 1), to continue to instruct the gods after he departs. He then leaves Tushita Heaven to take form as a human child in an Indian queen, Mahamaya (chapter 2). After a painless and productive time spent teaching the gods from within his mother's womb, he emerges into this world in a virgin birth from his mother's right side (chapter 3). His first triumphant words as a baby suggest that the infant is certain of his future as a religious leader, while the predictions of the royal sages foretell that he is destined to become a great ruler. Whether he is to become a great king or a great religious master remains a matter of narrative tension, however, as the young hero seems to forget his preordained calling to the spiritual life. The young prince lives in the lap of luxury among his coterie of women, enjoying love, marriage, learning, the arts, and athletics—all of which he holds complete mastery over (chapters 4 and 5). Revulsion at these indulgences deep in the pleasures of the senses leads to the key moment in the Bodhisattva's young spiritual career, renunciation; chapter 6 treats his daring escape from the palace, and his refusal to fulfill the obligations of his station in life as a prince. Once away from the palace and ensconced within the wild of the forest, he begins to meditate. He begins by performing austerities—strenuous practices of mental and physical contemplative practice and self-denial—that inflict such profound injury to his body and his mind that he is unable to concentrate his mind at all, much less meditate (chapter 7). After six years he abandons these exhausting and ultimately futile self-defeating practices after he nearly drops from exhaustion and malnourishment, and sets about to find equilibrium between asceticism and overindulgence that will allow him to develop his mind.

The Bodhisattva makes his final journey as an unenlightened being in chapter 8 when he walks to Bodhgaya, the site of his eventual realization under the Bodhi tree. But before this can happen he has one final task, an epic battle with the demon Mara, the personification of the fundamental challenges to human happiness: hatred, greed, and ignorance (chapter 9). After vanquishing Mara and his army, in a single, final night he completes the task that he set for himself eons ago, nothing less than a revolution in understanding. In the morning he sits, beholding the dawn's light with joyful, simple awareness (chapter 10). The Bodhisattva, now "the Buddha," rests with his hard-won achievement for a time, then embarks upon a forty-year teaching career that creates the Buddhist tradition (chapter 11). And yet, in the space of only a chapter, this career is over, and as he nears death, "the final passage from suffering," he bequeaths his teachings to his son, his close disciples, and all those who are ready to carry his tradition throughout India (chapter 12).

The life of the Buddha in twelve acts has a long and rich history in Tibetan literature, stretching back centuries before the time of Tenzin Chögyel. Most Tibetan historians trace the form to the second-century Indian writer Nagarjuna, perhaps the most famous classical Indian Buddhist philosopher. Nagarjuna is best known for his work on the central concern of all Buddhist philosophy, the insubstantiality, or "emptiness," of physical and psychological reality. His fame as a philosopher and writer was so great for Tibetan intellectuals that just about any work could gain authority if attributed to him, and this is likely what happened with a short work in verse on the twelve acts of the Buddha. More historically cautious Tibetan intellectuals attributed the poem to the twelfth-century writer Jikten Gönpo. Be that as it may, the poem urges its readers to feelings of faith and humility that should, ideally, accompany the recollection of the Buddha's career. Nagarjuna's "Praise to the Twelve Acts" is included at the conclusion of *The Life of the Buddha*.

THE LIFE OF THE BUDDHA
BY TENZIN CHÖGYEL

The present work offers a translation of one of the most engaging retellings of the Buddha's story in any language. It was composed in the middle of the eighteenth century, more than two millennia after the life of the

Buddha Shakyamuni, by a prominent Bhutanese intellectual, Tenzin Chögyel (in Tibetan, Rje Mkhan po Bstan
'dzin chos rgyal), who lived from 1701 to 1767. The full
title of Tenzin Chögyel's work is *The Life of the Lord
Victor Shakyamuni, Ornament of One Thousand Lamps
for the Fortunate Eon*. We may simply call it *The Life of
the Buddha* and it is presented here in its entirety.

Tenzin Chögyel was a prominent leader in the Drukpa
Kagyu ('Brug pa Bka' brgyud) school of Buddhism in
Bhutan. He is most famous today in Bhutan for his service to the state as the tenth Lord Abbot (Rje Mkhan
po)—the highest ecclesiastical authority—of Bhutan
from 1755 to 1762 and for his influential history of Bhutan, *The Religious History of the South* (*Lho'i chos
'byung*), which he completed in 1759. He was ordained
as a novice monk at the age of twelve in 1712, and
received a first-class monastic education. By the time he
was thirty-two he held major offices within the Bhutanese religious hierarchy, serving in the major religious
and political centers of Bhutan—the palaces at Punakha
and Wangdu, Tango Monastery, and elsewhere. He rose
to the peak of the religious hierarchy in Bhutan when he
was fifty-five years old, when he became responsible for
the religious affairs of the state as Lord Abbot of Bhutan.
In 1762, after eight years of government service, he
retired from office and lived his final years in retreat.

Tenzin Chögyel was a prominent author in Bhutan's
golden age of literary creativity. Although he was not the
most prolific writer among the Lord Abbots of Bhutan—
this distinction goes to his predecesssor, the ninth Lord
Abbot, Shakya Rinchen (1710–1759, Lord Abbot from
1745 to 1755)—by the time he was twenty-seven years of
age, he was already a major biographer, having composed a lengthy narrative on the life of his teacher Tenzin
Döndrup (1680–1728) upon the latter's death. He wrote

several other works of narrative literature, a history of the Bhutanese state, and beautiful poetic liturgical works for monasteries and temples in central Bhutan.

In its original Tibetan-language form, Tenzin Chög-yel's *Life of the Buddha* runs one hundred pages. Here in English it runs about the same. It is a brief work, and this is one of its most useful features, for it can easily be read in a sitting. Tenzin Chögyel's story may be one of hundreds of Buddha narratives produced in classical Tibetan during the last millennium, but it is one in a million if one considers this Bhutanese writer's talent for balancing brevity and completeness, description and action, poetic flourish and prosaic energy. There is little doubt that he wrote the work for Buddhist novices, young monks who needed to learn the basic arc of their founder's life without digression into the myriad details of doctrine to which close investigation into the philosophical implications of the Buddha's quest inevitably leads. Yet Tenzin Chögyel writes with a style that transcends his time and place while still retaining classical features of Buddhist narratives. What is perhaps most impressive about this short work is how it draws together the cosmic and the human. Tenzin Chögyel's *Life of the Buddha* is a story about the unfolding of good within the universe, and it is also a story of personal growth. It is a philosophical narrative on the nature of the cosmos and the relationship of human awareness to the infinite, yet it is also a story of personal relationships between fathers and sons, husbands and wives, teachers and students. We glimpse the majestic scale of the Buddha's epic journey toward enlightenment, a scale that exceeds the normal bounds of time, and stretches our imagination to worlds and realms across the universe. We also glimpse that scale in the smallest and most pervasive of human social relationships, the offering of a simple meal. It engages in us what the early pioneer of science fiction Olaf Stapledon referred to as "the hyper-telescopic imagination," that wonderful capacity to imagine in the same instant the minutest detail of earthly life together with the grandest vision of the heavens above. Tenzin Chögyel synthesizes the cosmic proportions of the Buddha's quest narrative with the drama of a single life as a simple human being as compellingly as any Tibetan-language writer before him or after.

The gods are key to this synthesis. Indra, Brahma, Vishnu, the four guardian kings, the serpent kings—gods are everywhere in the narrative, present and active in nearly every major event in the Buddha's life. This is one feature of Tenzin Chögyel's telling that will likely strike contemporary readers as unusual, for modernist narratives of the Buddha created today—and especially those created for Anglophone audiences in North America and Europe—simply leave out the gods, thereby insinuating that the Buddha achieved his goals with no help whatsoever. But this is far from the case; the success of the Buddha, one might say, was a celestial team effort. Tenzin Chögyel reminds us that the cast of characters in the Buddha's life contains a prominent troupe of heavenly figures. Indeed it is fair to say that Siddhartha would never have become the Buddha, that the human would never have transformed into the cosmic, without the persistent influence of a host of celestial influences.

Tenzin Chögyel uses another narrative element to punctuate the synthesis and the tension between the cosmic and the prosaic. A key feature of Tenzin Chögyel's narrative is his treatment of the Buddha's last days. Where other lives of the Buddha highlight the Buddha's final teachings, or emphasize the fact that the Buddha would have, could have lived longer if only his disciple Ananda had thought to ask him to remain on this earth for a while longer, Tenzin Chögyel brings the story of the Buddha to a close by reuniting him with his son, Rahula. This meeting of father and son, master and disciple, is a riveting, heart-wrenching scene that marks a memorable conclusion to the Buddha's life. It is also quite unusual among Tibetan-language lives of the Buddha, and must have come as a surprising twist to Tenzin Chögyel's readers. The Lord Abbot's other major work on the classic characters of Buddhism is his *Lives of the Sixteen Elders*. This collection of narratives begins with the story of the Buddha's son, Rahula. In a way, then, one could say that *Lives of the Sixteen Elders* begins with the very subject that *The Life of the Buddha* concluded with, although in fact the better part of Rahula's story centers on his life prior to meeting the Buddha. The story of Rahula is included here so that readers may learn of Rahula's backstory.

Tenzin Chögyel wrote *The Life of the Buddha* to be read and enjoyed. Other life stories of the Buddha are meant to be studied; they contain endless references to scriptural sources, digressions on troublesome episodes in the Buddha's life, or elaborate navigations of divergent narrative trajectories. These works are for scholars. Other works are meant to dazzle readers with their fine poetry or fantastic scenes: They extol the good qualities of the Buddha in sonorous verse, or wax long on the beauty of heavenly realms, yet make passing reference to episodes alive with human drama and inspiration. Tenzin Chögyel is not wholly immune to these aspirations, but he chastens his telling of the story with short phrases, laconic dialogue, and a quick pace. He uses verse to punctuate prose, verse drawn largely from the *Living Out of the Game Scripture*. These verses recapitulate action first told in prose, giving the story a stately pace even in its brevity, and offering readers a chance to pause and reflect upon the acts of the Buddha as he works toward the climax of his quest—enlightenment under the Bodhi tree.

Tenzin Chögyel is not interested in teaching Buddhist doctrine to his readers. The story teaches, to be sure, but nearly always through the narrative rather than over it or against it. He respects the power of the narrative itself to engage his reader more deeply with the teachings of the Buddha, which he surely intends his audience to do upon reading his story. The four noble truths, karma, the nature of enlightenment, the possibility and necessity of personal development, the absolute need for compassion toward others in the face of human suffering—all of these basic Buddhist doctrines are exemplified through the Buddha's actions. This is true of all stories of the Buddha's life. Yet not all writers respected the power of this narrative to express Buddhism's core teachings. Such writers inevitably insert discourses on Buddhist ideas that would have been better left to philosophical treatises. It is to Tenzin Chögyel's credit that he remains committed to letting the narrative push the doctrine, never allowing the excitement of the Buddha's life become mired in dogma.

SOURCES AND SCOPE

Tenzin Chögyel's *Life of the Buddha* is structured according to the standard set of twelve acts, with a single chapter dedicated to each. The Lord Abbot could have had any number of sources at his disposal upon which to draw the general contours of his story. Scores of Buddha narratives were composed prior to his, and he could have read any one of them without its leaving its specific imprint upon the rendition of the story that he set to writing. As early as the first decades of the ninth century, when the great translator Paltsek included the story of the Buddha in one of the first Tibetan anthologies of Buddhist teachings, his *Treatise on Scripture and Shakya*

Genealogy, Tibetan writers were retelling the rich yet unwieldy narratives of the Buddha's life contained in Indian Buddhist canonical literature in briefer, more approachable renderings. Major life stories began to appear in the twelfth century, when a major figure in the early Sakya school of western Tibet, Sönam Tsemo, appended a Buddha narrative to his *Introduction to Buddhism* (1147). Stand-alone lives of the Buddha also appeared during this time, though most of these remain lost or inaccessible in the massive archives of Tibetan literature in China, so we can glean little regarding their content and style save by comparison to known works. The fourteenth through seventeenth centuries all witnessed the publication of major lives of the Buddha, works that are still read today. Tibet's foremost classical historian, Butön Rinchendrup (1290–1364), wrote two lives of the Buddha, one a long anthology-style work drawing from Indian Buddhist vinaya literature (1354), the other a lengthy section in his *History of Buddhism* (1322). The most famous life of the Buddha was composed in 1434 (or 1494) by Nanam Tsünpa, about whom we know little despite the fact that his lengthy work constituted one of the major contributions to the genre up to that point and was printed in every quarter of Tibet in the centuries that followed. A last great classical work was composed in the early decades of the seventeenth century by Taranatha (1575–1634), a brilliant and innovative philosopher and writer whose legacy in western Tibet fell along with the losing parties of the Tibetan civil war in 1642. Both Nanam Tsünpa and Taranatha organized the Buddha's career into one hundred and twenty-five episodes, a far cry from the standard twelve. The additions are for the most part to the period of the Buddha's teaching, a forty-year period that receives abbreviated treatment in most twelve-act stories.

Tenzin Chögyel certainly knew a great deal of this literature. He displays a comfortable ease with the classical Indian sources that could only come from a deep and abiding engagement with the literary tradition as a whole. This is apparent in the sources from which he draws that were not the stock-in-trade among earlier writers. Yet for the majority of his work he relies on only a handful of well-chosen sources. In the conclusion he tells the reader something about his sources: "I abridged the words of the Buddha himself in the *Living Out of the Game Scripture,* without fabricating anything. For the episode in which the Transcendent One [the Buddha] enters nirvana I have relied upon the *White Lotus of Compassion Scripture,* and the *Great Final Nirvana Scripture.*" But he does not tell us everything about his sources here. Careful scrutiny of the classical Buddhist literature he quotes, and text-critical analysis of unstated parallel passages between his work and that of his predecessors, reveal that he relied upon works that he has not listed among his sources. For Tenzin Chögyel uses two famous works to tell the larger part of the Buddha's life, one unusual source to forge an emotionally charged conclusion, and another, also an unusual choice, to embellish the story with elegant verse. The first and most important of these is none other than Butön's *History of Buddhism.* Butön's history was the single most famous history of Buddhism in India among Tibetan intellectuals of all schools. The work economically presents an introduction to Buddhist models for learning, a life story of the Buddha, a history of the Buddhist tradition in South Asia from the death of the Buddha to its effective demise at the dawn of the thirteenth century, a brief account of the origins and early development of the tradition in Tibet, and a survey of Buddhist scriptures translated from Sanskrit into Tibetan. Butön's work is a model of scholastic writing, brimming with quote after quote from Buddhist scriptures, entertaining historical arguments, and theological queries, and it is ever willing to sidestep criticism by posing rhetorical questions only to offer the "correct" answer. This is the treatise's great strength as a work of Buddhist doctrine, and it is its great downfall as a compelling work of literature.

Tenzin Chögyel was well aware of this. Butön's *History of Buddhism* provided the Bhutanese writer with a complete and expertly planned life of the Buddha, yet one so laden with philosophical and source-critical digression as to make it all but unreadable for anyone but a highly trained scholar. Here was the perfect blueprint for a life of the Buddha, but an all too imperfect realization of that blueprint. Tenzin Chögyel makes liberal use of both the form and the content of Butön's *History,* as the cross-references in the notes to the translation should make clear. This is no mere copy, however, for Tenzin Chögyel wields a heavy editorial pen over Butön's writing, smoothing out awkward phrasing, excising digressions from the narrative, and removing needless scriptural citations. Where Butön spends five pages summarizing the debates over the actual place where the Buddha achieved enlightenment—here on earth or in one or more heavenly realms—Tenzin Chögyel pauses briefly for two lines to make the reader aware of the debates, and then moves on. Where Butön glosses over the final days of the Buddha's life, Tenzin Chögyel lingers in these emotion-filled moments, inviting readers to imagine, to feel the wrenching sadness at the master's passing.

In fact, Tenzin Chögyel leaves Butön's account at the Buddha's enlightenment and goes in search of other sources. One work he makes passing reference to, the *Scripture on the Great Passage from Suffering,* is the classic account of the Buddha's death for Tibetan authors.

Yet he bases the larger part of his accounts of the Buddha's death upon several lesser-known Buddhist scriptures, the most important of which for him is the *White
Lotus of Great Compassion Scripture,* a Mahayana
scripture detailing the Buddha's final teachings to divine
and human disciples.

The more immediate context for Tenzin Chögyel's work
is the literary and institutional scene of mid-eighteenth-
century Bhutan. His *Life of the Buddha* appears to be the
first brief retelling by a Bhutanese writer, though there
were certainly biographies written in the decades leading
up to his time. His immediate predecessor as Lord Abbot
of Bhutan, Shakya Rinchen, was a tireless biographer of
eminent Indian, Tibetan, and Bhutanese Buddhist masters. He wrote liturgies for the Buddha and his close disciples, the Sixteen Elders, but no narrative works dedicated
to these early Buddhist figures. The major biography in
Bhutan at the time was authored by a Tibetan living in
Bhutan in the mid-seventeenth century, though this
sprawling work could not be more different from Tenzin
Chögyel's taut retelling. Tsang Khenchen Pelden Gyatso
(1610–1684), a central Tibetan intellectual exiled in Bhutan after the fall of his supporters in the Tibetan civil war
of 1642, compiled a massive life story of almost one thousand densely packed pages. This is perhaps the largest life
of the Buddha in Tibetan. It is a veritable encyclopedia of
Buddha-lore, with citations from seemingly every con-
ceivable scriptural source that touches upon the Buddha's
story. It is possible that Tenzin Chögyel utilized Tsang
Khenchen's life of the Buddha more directly than is at
first apparent, for he used the same Tibetan writer's life of
Zhabdrung Nawang Namgyel, founder of the Bhutanese
state, in writing his own, more concise history of religion
and politics in Bhutan. In the end, however, Tsang
Khenchen wrote a reference work on the Buddha's life,

and it was left to Tenzin Chögyel to transform the story into an engrossing work of literature.

THE TRANSLATION

Tenzin Chögyel's life story of the Buddha is available in a single handwritten manuscript produced in Bhutan. He wrote in classical Tibetan, a form of Tibetan that is found throughout the Tibetan Buddhist world. In contemporary Bhutan, classical Tibetan is referred to as Chöké (chos skad), or "the language of Dharma," the language of Buddhism. It is thus most fitting to refer to the Lord Abbot's story of the Buddha as a work of Chöké, though in order to highlight its indebtedness to earlier, non-Bhutanese sources, it is also reasonable to identify his work as classical Tibetan. For it is indeed one of the wonders of the Tibetan Buddhist world that a reader trained in classical Tibetan could pick up a work written in this langage and read it quite easily, regardless of whether he or she was from Bhutan, Tibet, China, Mongolia, Russia, or wherever Tibetan Buddhist higher education flourished. Tenzin Chögyel was a Bhutanese writer through and through, yet he participated in a shared classical heritage that stretched across Asia.

Tenzin Chögyel completed his work in 1740, this much we know. Beyond that we do not know exactly where or when in Bhutan this particular manuscript of his work was produced, or if there were multiple copies made (though it is reasonable to presume that there were). It is possible that the manuscript was produced at Wangdu Phodrang, the fortress where Tenzin Chögyel wrote the work, though the many fires that have plagued the fortress through the centuries—including a disastrous one in 2012—may make it impossible ever to know this with certainty.

The manuscript is one hundred and five pages, with five lines per page. It is a simply produced manuscript, with no illustrations and few decorative motifs. The anonymous scribe produced Tenzin Chögyel's work in the üchen (dbu can) script, "the script with a head," referring to the uniform horizontal line at the top of each letter. This script is normally used for works produced as woodblock prints, though in Bhutan it was common practice to produce clean, readable handwritten manuscripts in üchen rather than one of the various cursive scripts used throughout the Tibetan Buddhist cultural world. The manuscript also includes a companion piece, *Lives of the Sixteen Elders,* which tells the stories of a famous set of disciples closest to the Buddha. When the manuscript was produced, these two works were considered to be a paired set, for their volume markings are Ka and Kha respectively, the first two letters of the Tibetan alphabet.

Those wishing to read the life story in the original Tibetan will find the corresponding pages of the Tibetan text in the notes. The notes also include references to the original Tibetan works and alternate English translations for every verse quoted by Tenzin Chögyel. Additionally, the notes systematically refer the reader to parallel scenes in the major Indian scriptural life of the Buddha, the *Living Out of the Game Scripture,* as well as in Butön's *History of Buddhism.* The original Tibetan text contains no subheadings beyond the twelve chapters. I have added subheadings within each chapter to ease the reader's course through the work. The life story moves along episodically, sometimes moving in rapid succession from one time and place to another, and it is useful to see these divisions clearly marked out. I have not used diacritics in this translation: Specialists may look to John Strong's *The Buddha: A Short Biography* or Robert Buswell and

Donald Lopez's *The Princeton Dictionary of Buddhism* for diacritical renderings of Sanskrit terms.

I have savored Tenzin Chögyel's rendition of this world-famous narrative as I have translated it. It is a powerful story that has the potential to engage people across cultures at a deeply emotional level, a simple, human level. This was brought home to me when I read portions of the final meeting of the Buddha and his son, Rahula, at an international gathering in Thimphu, the capital city of Bhutan. I knew that the story of the Buddha would be well known to my audience, and I was nervous that the variant story of Rahula's meeting with his dying father would provoke some controversy or dismissal of Tenzin Chögyel's liberty with certain elements of the narrative. I could not have been more wrong. Instead the emotional gravity of integrating the death of Shakyamuni as teacher with his death as a father reached out to people in the audience in ways I had not imagined it would. At the close of the reading a woman from Malaysia who was about my age came up to me to talk about Tenzin Chögyel's conclusion to the Buddha's life. I thought she might want to talk about the literary history of the work, or compare this version of the story to versions she knew from her country, but her concerns were not literary or academic. The death of the Buddha had brought her to tears and she stood before me weeping. "Before I came to Thimphu," she said, "I was taking care of my elderly father back home in Malaysia. I am not sure if he will still be alive when I get home. When I heard the story of Rahula's difficulty in saying good-bye to his father, I thought, 'This is just like my life. I am Rahula, wishing he did not have to say good-bye to his father, and my father is the Buddha, telling me it is okay to say good-bye.'" I hope that readers of this translation

will appreciate the skill with which this Bhutanese writer
has told this ancient tale, in a way that brims with immediate relevance to our lives today, whoever and wherever
we may be.

KURTIS R. SCHAEFFER

Suggestions for Further Reading

There are quite a few life stories of Shakyamuni available in English, even if few translations of traditional biographies have been published in recent generations. These may be conveniently grouped into two categories: summaries or overviews produced in English by contemporary Anglophone scholars, and translations of works composed in a number of Asian languages and translated into English. The present work, of course, falls in the latter category. The readings suggested here include examples of both, as well as other general works that will form useful starting points for exploring the life of the Buddha and its implications in greater detail. John Strong's *The Buddha: A Short Biography* offers extensive bibliographic references to stories of the Buddha. Any reader interested in learning more about the Buddha's life should consult Strong's book.

Aśvaghoṣa. *The Life of the Buddha*. Translated by Patrick Olivelle. New York: New York University Press and JJC Foundation, 2008. Second-century CE Indian writer Aśvaghoṣa composed the first complete story of the Buddha, from birth to death. This work was translated from Sanskrit into Tibetan (and Chinese), though it never had the influence that the *Lalitavistara Sūtra,* or the *Living Out of the Game Scripture,* did among Tibetan authors. E. H. Johnston, in *The Buddhacarita or Acts of the Buddha*

(Calcutta: Baptist Mission Press, 1936), includes a translation from Tibetan and Chinese of the latter portion up to the Buddha's death.

Bays, Gwendolyn, translator. *The Voice of the Buddha: The Beauty of Compassion*. Berkeley, CA: Dharma Publishing, 1983. Two volumes. A complete translation of the French translation of the *Living Out of the Game Scripture, or Lalitavistara Sūtra*: P. E. Foucaux, *Rgya Tch'er Rol Pa; Ou, Développement des Jeux, Contenant L'histoire du Bouddha Çakya-mouni: Traduit sur la Version Tibétaine du Bkah Hgyour, et Revu sur L'original Sanscrit (Lalitavistâra)*. Paris: L'Imprimerie Royale, 1847. The *Lalitavistara Sūtra* was a major source for the present version of *The Life of the Buddha*. Parallel passages are cited in the notes of the present work.

Beal, Samuel. *The Romantic Legend of Śākya Buddha: A Translation of the Chinese Version of the Abhiniṣkramaṇasūtra*. London: Trübner & Co., 1875. Beal translates a circa sixth-century Chinese work that begins with Buddha's original vow and ends in the midst of his teaching career.

Bhikkhu Ñāṇamoli. *The Life of the Buddha: According to the Pali Canon*. Onalaska, WA: BPS Pariyatti Editions, 1992. An anthology of passages from the Buddhist canon in Pāli, arranged to tell the life story of Shakyamuni from birth through death and up to the first council.

Bigandet, P. *The Life, or Legend of Gaudama, the Budha of the Burmese*. Rangoon: American Mission Press, 1866. A lengthy and detailed Burmese retelling of the Buddha's story from his original vow through death.

Buswell, Robert E., Jr., and Donald S. Lopez Jr. *The Princeton Dictionary of Buddhism*. Princeton: Princeton University Press, 2014. A major reference work for the study of Buddhism. See especially the entries for Buddha, *Lalitavistara*, Śākyamuni, Twelve Deeds of the Buddha.

Foucher, Alfred. *The Life of the Buddha: According to the Ancient Texts and Monuments of India*. Translated by Simone Brangier Boas. Middletown, CT: Wesleyan University Press, 1963. An abridged translation of Foucher's

1949 *La Vie du Bouddha,* in which he utilizes Indian sources to synthesize a narrative of the Buddha's life from pre-birth to death.

Hesse, Hermann. *Siddhartha: An Indian Tale.* Translated by Joachim Neugroschel. New York: Penguin Books, 1999. Hesse's novel chronicles the story of Siddhartha, a young man in search of life's meaning in ancient India. Siddhartha meets the Buddha on his quest and ultimately decides not to follow him in favor of forging his own vision of personal liberation. Although the Buddha is not the central character in *Siddhartha,* Hesse's work has sparked interest in the Buddha, Buddhism, and Indian religions worldwide ever since its publication in Germany in 1922, and especially since Hilda Rosner's English translation of 1951 was published in North America.

Jamgön Kongtrul Lodrö Tayé. *The Treasury of Knowledge, Books Two, Three, Four: Buddhism's Journey to Tibet.* Translated by Ngawang Zangpo. Ithaca: Snow Lion Publications, 2010. Pages 43–90 offer a scholastically oriented presentation of the Twelve Deeds of the Buddha.

Jayawickrama, N. A. *The Story of Gotama Buddha (Jātakanidāna).* Oxford: The Pali Text Society, 2002. A translation from the Pāli language, this story is an introduction to a collection of narratives of the Buddha's previous lives.

Kerouac, Jack. *Wake Up: A Life of the Buddha.* New York: Penguin Books, 2008. A modern prose retelling of the Buddha's life, based in great part upon Aśvaghoṣa's *Life of the Buddha.*

Kohn, Sherab Chödin. *A Life of the Buddha.* Boston: Shambhala Publications, 2009. Previously published in 1994 as *The Awakened One,* this is a contemporary retelling of the Buddha's life from original vow to death, based primarily on Bhikkhu Nyanamoli's *Life of the Buddha,* Bays's *Voice of the Buddha,* and Johnston's translation of the *Buddhacarita.*

Lang, David Marshall. *The Wisdom of Balahvar: A Christian Legend of the Buddha.* London: George Allen and Unwin, 1957. This is a good place to start if one wants to learn of the fascinating transformation of Buddhist narratives in medieval Christian literature.

Lewis, Todd T., and Subarna Man Tuladhar, translators. *Sugata Saurabha: An Epic Poem from Nepal of the Life of the Buddha, by Chittadhar Hṛdaya.* New York: Oxford University Press, 2010. An epic poem composed in the mid-1940s by Nepal's greatest twentieth-century poet.

Lopez, Donald S., Jr. *The Story of Buddhism.* San Francisco: Harper San Francisco, 2001. A reliable and entertaining introduction to the Buddhist traditions of Asia. Chapter 2 surveys the life, teachings, and doctrinal issues relating to the figure of the Buddha.

_____. *Buddhist Scriptures.* New York: Penguin Books, 2004. An anthology of passages from Buddhist literature throughout Asia, including several texts dealing with the life and death of the Buddha on pages 101–220.

Malalasekera, G. P. *Dictionary of Pāli Proper Names.* London: Murray, 1937. Two volumes. A useful reference work for studying the many characters in narratives of the Buddha's life.

Nakamura, Hajime. *Gotama Buddha: A Biography Based upon the Most Reliable Texts.* Translated by Gaynor Sekimori. Tokyo: Kōsei Publishing Co., 2000–2005. Two volumes. An extensive comparative and synthetic study of nonbiographical Indian sources for the story of the Buddha.

Nawano, Nikkyo. *Shakyamuni Buddha: A Narrative Biography.* Tokyo: Kōsei Publishing Co., 1969. A brief retelling of the Buddha's story from birth to death, based upon Indian sources.

Nhat Hanh, Thich. *Old Path, White Clouds: Walking in the Footsteps of the Buddha.* Translated by Mobi Ho. Berkeley, CA: Parallax Press, 1991. A lengthy contemporary Vietnamese retelling of the Buddha's life that deemphasizes miraculous elements of the story in order to emphasize existential and social messages.

Padma chos 'phel (Pema Chöpel). *Leaves of the Heaven Tree: The Great Compassion of the Buddha*. Translated by Debora Black. Berkeley, CA: Dharma Publishing, 1997. A translation of a nineteenth-century Tibetan prose retelling of the famous *Bodhisattvāvadanakalpalatā, A Vine of Tales About the Bodhisattva* by the eleventh-century Kashmirian poet Kṣemendra. Kṣemendra's work was famous in Tibet, and served as inspiration for finely crafted poetic narratives throughout the centuries. Its 108 narratives include many episodes from the Buddha's life.

Penner, Hans H. *Rediscovering the Buddha: Legends of the Buddha and Their Interpretation*. New York: Oxford University Press, 2009. Penner retells the story of the Buddha based primarily upon the Pali Text Society's translations of the Pāli-language scriptural collection.

Rockhill, William Woodville. *The Life of the Buddha Derived from Tibetan Works in the Bkah-Hgyur and Bstan-Hgyur*. London: Trübner & Co., 1884. A major early work on the story of the Buddha, consisting primarily of a summary of the story from the Tibetan translation of the Sanskrit *Mūlasarvāstivāda Vinaya*, the monastic code of the Indian Mūlasarvāstivāda school, compiled in the first or second century CE.

Strong, John. *The Buddha: A Short Biography*. Oxford: One-World Publications, 2001 (reissued in 2009 as *The Buddha: A Beginner's Guide*). A concise yet major reference work for anyone interested in the life of the Buddha and the vast and varied versions of the Buddha narrative that were created throughout Asia. This is essential reading.

Taranatha. *Le Soleil de la Confiance: La Vie du Bouddha*. Translated into French by the Padmakara Translation Committee. Saint-Léon-sur-Vézère: Éditions Padmakara, 2003. *The Sun of Faith* is one of the largest and most detailed life stories of the Buddha authored in Tibet. Taranatha (1575–1634) was a master of Indian history and literature. He based his retelling of the Buddha's life on the early Indian monastic conduct literature, a departure for Tibetan authors, who typically relied upon the *Lalitavistara Sūtra*.

Tsangnyön Heruka. *The Life of Milarepa*. Translated by Andrew Quintman. New York: Penguin Books, 2010. The fifteenth-century Tibetan writer Tsangnyön Heruka employs the framework of the twelve acts of the Buddha to tell the story of Tibet's most famous hermit-saint, Milarepa.

The Life of
the Buddha

PROLOGUE

To you who see all things I pray.
I pray to you always with body, speech, and mind,
My faith strengthened by a hundred
Recollections of the reality of your being.
I seek the place where Buddhas reside,
I find no happiness in this chain of lives.

Lord. Transcendent One. Vanquisher. Fully Awakened.
Learned. Virtuous. Gone in Bliss. World Wise. Unsur-
passed Charioteer. Guide for Living Beings. Teacher of
Gods. Teacher of Humans. Peerless King of the Shakyas.
Lion of the Shakyas. Great Sage of the Shakyas.

In faith I prostrate to you. I touch my head to your
immaculate feet. In you I seek refuge.

Reveal your face to me, Transcendent One, in every
life I live! Extend your golden hand to touch my head, to
bless me.

Best of Victors, Friend of the Sun, the Light of Love—
You rise above all other brilliant Victors.
In every realm the Victors speak as one of your wondrous
   tales.
To you I bow.
The light of your name, Protector, touches me,
And I awake from the sleep of unknowing.

It offers an unmatched spectacle in which understanding
   flourishes,
And nurtures countless disciples to the end. Wonderful!
You purify this Buddha realm and sustain the practice of
   enlightenment.
You are a sign of courage for a thousand famous heroes,
A moon rising in the center of the stars.
You bring a sigh of relief even to those Victors' sons who
   have yet to come.
The Victors of past, present, and future
Might speak for many eons,
And still not describe one drop of the ocean of the
   Buddha's merits.
So how can a simple person like me ever hope to
   know you?
And when I dream of being virtuous
The rhythm of the Lord Subduer's supreme golden body
Comes naturally to mind—I do not create it.
Buddha, is this a karmic trace of knowing you once?
Precious Teacher, you are a singular
Object of faith and undivided recollection.
So as an aid for recollecting you,
I have composed this life story, summarized from all the
   scriptures.

CHAPTER ONE

HEAVEN

ERAS OF THE UNIVERSE

There are Eras of Light.

There are Eras of Darkness.

In Eras of Light a Buddha appears.

In Eras of Darkness no Buddha appears.

In an Era of Light, the Era of Good, one thousand or one thousand and five Buddhas appear. After this there are sixty Eras of Darkness. After this comes the Era of Light called the Great Renown, during which ten thousand Buddhas appear. After ten thousand Great Eras of Darkness pass, the Era of Light called the Starlike Era comes, during which eighty thousand Buddhas appear. After this come three hundred Eras of Darkness, and after this comes the Era of Light known as the Array of Good Qualities, during which eighty-four thousand Buddhas appear. This is all taught in the *Scripture of the Era of Good*.

The appearance of the Buddha in this world is extremely rare. So at this very moment you must make an effort to learn. Contemplate. Meditate.

THE HUMAN PREDICAMENT

Now, living beings are like the sky. They are limitless. Every living being is in essence naturally luminous. Every living being possesses the enlightened heart of Buddha. And yet the truth of this is obscured by a dim unknowing. Ethical cause and effect causes us to accumulate many greater and lesser mental attitudes. And because of this we uncontrollably experience every manner of grief. Given the unending nature of cyclic existence, such living beings experience this continually, crying out for mercy, "Kyema! Alas!"

A wonder it is that ignorance,
Deludes living beings, and so,
They forget the suffering of loss,
While craving more possessions.

The snake is pleased resting in his hole,
He flicks his poison tongue, saying nothing.
Proud fools rest ever in their errors,
Saying senseless things in greed, hatred, and ignorance.

Just so, we are predisposed toward the mental perspectives of ethical cause and effect. From these perspectives we cling to things as if they were inherently real, and it is difficult to overcome such habitual patterns of confusion. Because of this, the realms of living beings are without end, and we become the perfect carriers of all manner of actions, both good and evil.

In these realms, the only firm source of joy, the only protector, the only island, the only holy refuge, is the Buddha together with his spiritual sons. Because of this, living beings who seek refuge in the Buddha after simply hearing his name come to the end of their negative life states.

The Pig's Tale says,

> Who goes for refuge in Buddha,
> Never takes a bad rebirth.
> If you leave a god's body,
> A god's body you'll take again.

Even so, unless a Buddha comes into this world and teaches the Dharma, you may live for a hundred eras, you may thrive and search, and you still will not even come across the mere mention of the Buddha. There is a saying about this in a tale of the previous lives of the Vanquisher: For a single verse, Buddha pierced his body one billion times with an iron lance.

" 'Buddha'—even the word is so rare in the world!" said the Teacher himself.

Given all this, I recalled at great length the good qualities of the Buddha. I thought that if unbiased people of humble origins were to simply hear the name of the Buddha, this would be greatly beneficial. So I was eager to compose a brief life story of the precious, compassionate Teacher. This turned out to be a very good thing to do.

The *Praise in One Hundred and Fifty Verses* says,

> If you are a thinking being,
> Go to seek refuge in him.
> Offer praise and veneration,
> Live by his teachings, this is right.

The *Praise Exceeding the Gods* also says,

> Heartfelt faith, and joy as well,
> Doubt toward others, these are right.
> Whoever reveres this one, Buddha,
> Obtains the perfect bliss of Gods.

The good qualities of the Buddha run wide and deep. I am unable to describe them. Still, I will provide a small foundation for your faith, upon which you may remember the Lord of Dharma, this powerful sage, deep in your heart, down in your bones.

THE ORIGINAL VOW OF THE BUDDHA

I will speak a little about the Buddha for those living beings who share the same lot as myself.

When he was just a bodhisattva, this Teacher of ours made a vow surpassing that of all the Victors and their spiritual sons, all the best of swans. He had strength of heart. His endurance was great. He knew the means to shepherd living beings. And if he was able to accomplish this much in the past, what reason is there even to speak of his vow now that he has achieved manifest and complete enlightenment?

Now, this have I heard: These Lords, these Buddhas, first make a vow to attain supreme enlightenment. They then collect wisdom and merit for three incalculable eras. Finally they achieve awakening. This is the reality of things.

Long ago, in a time countless eras past, our Buddha came into the presence of the completely perfect Buddha, the Transcendent One named Lord Ratnagarbha, the Jewel Heart.

"One thousand Buddhas have appeared in this Era of Good," our Buddha said. "Yet, though they practice the conduct of bodhisattvas, every one of those bodhisattvas has committed to their own realm for a mere seven years.

"The other sons of Victors made commitments only to those realms that were pure. They abandoned this world of unbearable suffering, with its five corruptions—corrupt living, attitudes, emotions, people, and times. The other sons of Victors cast this world away, leaving it to the Era of Darkness."

BUDDHA'S PREVIOUS LIVES

Then this Teacher of ours took birth as the brahmin Samudrarenu. With his great love he took this impure world for his own. And for this world he made five hundred magnificent prayers of aspiration. In time he fulfilled his ambitions, for he was prophesied to possess a strength of heart greater than every other Buddha, as well as compassion surpassing all others. In time he did achieve this.

This is how the Bodhisattva's initial development of the enlightened attitude is explained in the *Scripture of the White Lotus of Compassion*. The *Scripture of the Era of Good* describes it differently:

> When I was in a lowly earlier life,
> To him, to Shakyamuni, the Transcendent One,
> I made an offering of all things fine,
> And set my mind upon enlightenment.

The *Scripture of Returning Kindness*, the *Scripture of the White Lotus of Compassion*, and the *Scripture of the Three Collections* all say this: The Buddha was once the son of a potter, and his name was Prabhasa. He offered a clay pot, five shells, a pair of boots, and a parasol to Great Shakyamuni Buddha. And he made a vow:

"One Gone Thus, may I become like you."

With these words he developed the intention to become enlightened, and from this vow he achieved enlightenment. This process is explained in both the traditions of the Learners and of the Great Way.

THE INTENTION TO BECOME
ENLIGHTENED

When the Bodhisattva was born as King Prasannakirti, he relied upon learning to tame an elephant and cultivated his intention to become enlightened. From that time up to the era of Buddha Rashtrapala the Bodhisattva venerated seventy-five thousand Buddhas, completed the first immeasurable eon, and thereby attained the first spiritual plateau in the development of a bodhisattva.

Then he venerated seventy-six thousand Buddhas, from Buddha Sadhukara up through that of Indradvaja. He completed the second immeasurable eon, and thereby attained the second through the seventh plateaus.

From the era of Buddha Dipankara up through that of Buddha Kashyapa he venerated seventy-seven thousand Buddhas. He completed the third immeasurable eon, and attained the eighth plateau and beyond, all the way up to the eleventh plateau, the totally luminous plateau of Buddhahood.

The Bodhisattva attained the state of omniscient Buddhahood. It does not matter if you describe this in terms of the five paths and the six perfections or the three forms of understanding and the four applications of contemplative practice. The *Praise in One Hundred and Fifty Verses* says,

> To lead afflicted people out
> Of the depths of this miserable existence,
> There is nothing that you will not do,
> No means and no method at all.

Just so, through countless streams of rebirths such as King Prabhasa, Maitribhadra, and Chandraprabha, the Bodhisattva purified realms of existence, engaged living

beings in the necessary prerequisites for enlightenment, and
completed the performance of his prayers and aspirations.
And since our Teacher is of great strength and fortitude,
he continued on with this for another thirty immeasurable
eons, doing whatever was necessary.

The scripture just mentioned also says,

> Through three immeasurable eons you
> Made efforts such as this for them,
> With effort as your only friend,
> So you attain the highest state.

How did the Bodhisattva become a Buddha? If the essence
of enlightenment is considered to be a state of realization,
then in his final life the Bodhisattva transformed into a
body of enlightenment, which is infinitely luminous. If
the essence of enlightenment is considered to be a place,
then he became enlightened in the form of an enjoyment
body in the Gandavyuha Akanishta, or the realm of Buddha Vairochana.

Now, this particular realm of Akanishta is said to exist
above the ordinary Akanishta. Yet the Middle Teaching
says that it exists outside the realm of Pure Akanishta.
The Descent into Lanka Scripture says,

> Bedecked with jewels of every kind,
> Akanishta Heaven, land of joy,
> Highest of pure realms—living here
> The Buddha gained true Buddhahood,
> Emanated here he was awakened.

Master Vagishvarakirti explains,

> He knew the highest truth in Akanishta.
> As Shvetaketu he served the Tushita gods.

For people here he became Shakyamuni,
Beat the Lord of Death and showed miracles to all.
  Victory to him!

IN TUSHITA HEAVEN

It was through events such as these that the Bodhisattva
first appeared in Tushita Heaven as Shvetaketu, the holy
son of the gods. When Buddha Kashyapa journeyed to earth,
the Bodhisattva was anointed as his replacement and he
stayed in Tushita, teaching the Dharma to the gods.

Now, the Bodhisattva considered the following:

"In all the many lives," he thought, "I have lived to the
fullest, I have devoted my flesh, my head, my blood, my
wife, my child. I have quite renounced them. I have utterly
renounced them to live by the discipline of austerity. I
have done such things because I have developed compassion toward all living beings.

"Pity! This world has no one to guide it. It has no one to
protect it, no place to go for refuge. I will save those who
are not saved, who suffer from ignorance, poor mental
health, horrible circumstances, short life spans, and poor
health. I will set free those who are not free. I will give
relief to those who have no relief. I will liberate from suffering those who are not liberated from suffering."

He thought about this for a long time and decided that
the time to undertake these things was now.

And presently the Buddhas everywhere urged the gods,
and the Bodhisattva's previous aspiration prayers urged
them on as well. And the gods made music and begged
the Bodhisattva with these words.

"With virtues vast, you're mindful, understanding,
With unmatched cunning, wisdom shining bright.

With peerless strength and vast ability,
Consider Dipankara's prophecy!

The glory of your virtue, supreme being,
Beautifies the palace here in heaven.
Yet, if your heart is possessed of compassion,
Let it rain down like banners, sheets of love!"

Now, the sons of the gods in this Pure Land of Tushita
had transformed into brahmins twelve years before the
Bodhisattva was to enter his mother's womb.

"If the Bodhisattva enters the womb," they prophesied, "he will become either a universal monarch or a
Buddha." But this will be explained in more detail below.

"In twelve years the Bodhisattva will enter his mother's womb, and you shall quit this world," they said to
the self-enlightened ones.

One self-enlightened one named Matanga, who lived
on Golangagulaparivartana Hill near Rajagriha, heard
the sons of gods say this, and he passed away, leaving his
footprint on the mountain rock. At Varanasi five hundred self-enlightened ones immolated themselves and
passed away. Relics fell from the fire, so the place is called
Rishipatana, "Falling Sage."

Now, the Bodhisattva considered the exhortations of
the gods. And he beheld a place where people live for one
hundred years. This was Jambudvipa, the Rose Apple
Continent, in the Middle Country, among the royal classes.
He also considered the class, the times, the country, the
ancestry, and the women in this world as he prepared to
leave for the human world.

"I am leaving this place, Tushita Heaven, to become
the son of King Suddhodana." Three times he spoke to
the residents of Tushita Heaven and the six classes of
gods in the Realm of Desire.

"I will understand what is essential. You gods, whoever strives for what is essential must do so as a human
in the Middle Country."

"Please understand!" the gods of Tushita Heaven
begged him. "As it is now the world is covered with sin,
and not one person is ready for the teaching. The world
has been confused by eighteen extremist teachers and soph-
ists, such as Purana Kashyapa, Maskari Gocaliputra, and
the like."

Again the Bodhisattva spoke.

> "A single lion defeats a herd of beasts.
> A single diamond smashes many rocks.
> Indra bests the demon hordes alone.
> The one and only sun dispels all dark."

"Friends," he continued, "there are one hundred and
eight doors through which the Dharma appears. When a
Royal Son transmigrates, he must show these to people.

"Faith. This is the door through which the Dharma
appears in such a way that people will never cease to
contemplate it." And he continued to speak of the doors
of the Dharma.

"The land anointed by a Buddha," he concluded, "is the
door through which the Dharma appears, from his entry
into the womb to his great liberation from suffering."

> When from this supreme place of Tushita,
> That lion of a man, the Leader, left.

"Friends, the heedless life you must give up!" he said
to all the gods around him. And as he said these words
the Bodhisattva removed the crown from his head and
set it upon the head of Maitreya.

"Friends," he said, "this bodhisattva, Maitreya, will teach the Dharma to you."

And so anointing Maitreya as the leader of Tushita Heaven, Shvetaketu prepared to travel into our world.

The Ornament for the Thousand-Light Eon, the Life Story of Lord Victor Shakyamuni.

Act One.

How he first became intent upon reaching supreme enlightenment, gathered virtue and wisdom over three immeasurable eons, and became truly enlightened. After that, how he appeared as Shvetaketu and dwelt in Tushita Heaven.

CHAPTER TWO

DESCENT

Essence distilled from three well-performed eras,
One hundred qualities flourishing through the strength
    of wisdom,
Enlightenment's true heart, a font of virtue,
The glory of existence, I put my faith in you.

The Bodhisattva bestowed extensive Dharma teachings
to the gathering of gods. Then he asked them, "Friends,
in what form should I enter the womb of my mother?"

"It would be fitting," some said, "for you to enter in the
form of Brahma."

"He should enter in the form of the god Indra," said
others.

"According to the Vedas," said Agratejas, son of the
gods, "to come in the form of an elephant is proper."

Thereupon the Bodhisattva readied for departure, and
eighteen omens of his birth appeared in the city of Kapilavastu, within the palace of Suddhodana, king of the
Shakya family.

IN HIS MOTHER'S WOMB

Winter passed, and in the last month of spring, the stars
fell in the fourteenth lunar mansion. The time was right.

The Bodhisattva saw that the moment had come for him to become the best among the three realms of gods, humans, and subterranean spirits. He saw that the time had come for him to be honored by the world. On the fifteenth day, at midnight during the full moon, in the constellation Pushya, the Bodhisattva transferred from Tushita Heaven into the womb of his mother. At that moment she was undertaking purification rituals, and she imagined a white baby elephant with six gold-covered tusks, the complexion of his head was like a lattice of worms. Her arms and legs, her entire body, and her senses were without pain. The Bodhisattva then entered his mother on the right side. And after entering the womb he stayed on her right side.

The Bodhisattva's mother beheld the following in a dream. Her body and her mind became suffused with a great feeling of well-being.

> A cap of woven gold, a red crown,
> He had six tusks and was white,
> Like a shell, or snow, or silver.
> I felt a great elephant had come to me.
>
> He entered me, and my body and mind.
> Both became enraptured with bliss
> Unheard, unseen, not felt before.
> And I fell as if into a trance.

She asked the priests about these dream visions.

"A special son will come," they offered in prophecy, "and if he remains in the kingdom he will become a wheel-turning king. But if he renounces the kingdom, he will become enlightened."

And all the while the Bodhisattva stayed in his mother's

womb, he remained untouched by impurities, for he lived
inside a three-storied palace crafted from snake-essence
sandalwood. The palace was called the Jewel Array and
was for the enjoyment of the Conqueror's Child. Inside was
a comfortable cushioned throne, and all around this throne
the palace was filled with an endless variety of offerings
from the gods.

On the night that he entered his mother's womb, a
great land burst from the waters below to a height of six
million four hundred thousand leagues. And on this land
a magnificent lotus bloomed and rose all the way to
Brahma's world, whereupon there were one hundred thousand leaders and holy people. The Great Brahma had the
power to see the lotus, but no one else was able to see it.
In that lotus was placed all the vital elixir, the essence,
the sap of the three thousand realms, as a drop of nectar.
Brahma placed this in a beryl goblet and handed it to the
Bodhisattva. The Bodhisattva took pity on Brahma, so
he accepted the cup.

Then something happened that was beyond imagination. A great many bodhisattvas from every direction, as
well as all the gods, from the four guardian kings of the
Land of Desire to the Unsurpassed Gods of Land Without Form, came to request a teaching, and stayed to lis-
ten to it.

The Bodhisattva's mother, Mayadevi, also worshipped
him as he lived in her womb. And many different crowds
of gods worshipped him and requested a teaching. He
replied to their requests, and as they gazed upon him
they experienced innumerable feelings of joy, and thirty-
six billion gods and humans were brought to maturity
through the three styles of teaching.

And though he did this, maturing and liberating people in incredible numbers, no one, save the gods and the

people who shared their good fortune, were able to see this. And this was the reason that the Bodhisattva needed to enter into his mother's womb.

The Ornament for the Thousand-Light Eon, the Life Story of Lord Victor Shakyamuni.

Act Two.

How he descended from Tushita Heaven and entered the womb.

CHAPTER THREE

BIRTH

It is time for the Sun's Friend to rise,
From the ocean, the womb of Maya,
Time to lift the darkness from the living.
He made ready with merit,
He shines, no equal in this realm of life.

Now, the Bodhisattva stayed in his mother's womb for ten or twelve months. He experienced pleasure without end there. His mother, Mayadevi, then recognized that the time had come for the Bodhisattva to be born. She related this to King Suddhodana, and the king had the roads and the gardens swept clean and decorated with ornaments fit for the gods. Flowers bloomed and spread out, and there appeared thirty-two omens that something good was about to come.

THE BIRTH OF THE BUDDHA

Now, the queen had many gardens, yet she went to her garden in Lumbini. In due course she came to the precious Plaksha tree, the fig tree. This tree had long been a support for mothers of Buddhas in the past. The gods of pure realms pray to it even now.

Queen Maya came before the fig tree. The tree bowed and prayed to the Buddha's mother.

Mayadevi reached out with her right hand to grasp a branch of the tree. She looked up to the sky and yawned, and the Bodhisattva was born from her right side. She felt no pain. He was not dirty from the impurities of the womb, and he was fully dressed.

A host of gods scattered flowers about as he was born. The gods Brahma and Indra received him in a celestial muslin wrap. Two feathered fans and a parasol appeared in midair as the serpent kings Nanda and Upananda bathed him from the sky. He had lived in a many-storied palace within his mother's womb. But Brahma now whisked it away so that it might be worshipped in his own world.

THE SEVEN STEPS

As the Bodhisattva set foot upon the earth, a magnificent lotus sprang up and grew.

"Behold me!" he said to Indra. Atop these great lotuses he looked to the four directions with the gaze of a magnificent being.

And he took seven steps to the east.

"I will be the first of all human beings!" he said.

He stepped to the north.

"I will be worthy of offerings from gods and humans!"

He stepped to the west.

"I have become the best in this world!" he said. "This is my final life, for I have transcended birth, aging, and death."

He stepped to the south.

"I will be without equal among all living beings!" he said.

He looked down.

"I will overcome demons and their hordes!" he said.

A great rain of Dharma fell to put out the fires of hell that torment all the inhabitants of that realm, and they were soothed with well-being.

He looked up.

"I will be looked up to by all living beings!" he said.

And wherever he stepped a lotus sprang up, and this wide earth rumbled.

THE BODHISATTVA'S FAME

The appearance of his golden brilliance filled the earth, outshining even the likes of the sun and the moon. The reality of these inconceivable auspicious omens in this universe of one hundred million worlds is beyond words.

At this time it also so happened that four minor kings were born in the four great regions. Then five hundred noblemen were born. Ten thousand daughters were born, including Yashodhara. Eight hundred servant women were born. Five hundred bondsmen were born, including Chandaka. Ten thousand stallions were born, including Kantaka, and ten thousand mares. Five hundred cows were born, and five hundred bulls. And at the center of the continent the Bodhi tree was born, around which five hundred gardens and five hundred treasures arose.

And the son of the king was given the name Siddhartha, and he became renowned throughout the world.

THE DEATH OF MAYADEVI

After the Bodhisattva was born, his mother's right side returned to the way it was before his birth. And yet, seven days later she passed away and was reborn in the Heaven of the Thirty-Three Gods. The Bodhisattva was not the cause of her death, no! The Bodhisattva did not bring about her death. Yet when she beheld that her son would leave home, she died of a broken heart.

Then the Bodhisattva went to the temple of the family gods. Some people from the Shakya family were behaving rudely in the temple. He subdued them, and he became known as Shakyamuni, "the one who subdues the Shakya people." Shakyavardhana and the other temple gods bowed down to him.

The people praised him. "He is a god among gods!"

The young Shakyamuni was then given to the care of Prajapati. And he was also given to the care of thirty-two nursemaids. Eight cared for him on their laps. Eight suckled him at their breast. Eight played games with him. Eight cleaned the filth from him.

THE FIRST SAGE'S PREDICTION

Now, there was a sage living in the Himalaya Mountains whose name was Asita. This sage possessed five kinds of clairvoyance. Asita and his nephew Narada had visions of signs indicating the Bodhisattva's virtue. So, like kings of geese they flew to the city of Kapilavastu. They clasped their hands in prayer, prostrated, and walked clockwise around the Bodhisattva.

Asita took the Bodhisattva on his lap and considered him. He saw perfectly the characteristics of a great person and the markings of excellence upon the Bodhisattva. The Bodhisattva, Asita explained, would either remain at home and become a wheel-turning king or abandon home and become the Transcendent One. And he described the way in which he would become perfectly and completely enlightened.

After this, Asita offered a prophecy.

> "I see the omens of this newborn babe,
> Thirty-two good signs enhance his form."

And Asita continued,

> "His private parts, now hidden in a sheath,
> His topknot, these cannot be seen by all.
> So there is no way he will stay at home."

THE SECOND SAGE'S PREDICTION

Another scripture says that there was a sage named Arana living on Mount Sarvadhara. His grandson Agnidatta-pura had learned of the Bodhisattva's birth.

"Learned one," he asked his grandfather,

> "Have all of a thousand suns
> Shone at once right here, right now?
> This mountain and this rocky cave
> Are alight with such a single flame!"

Arana replied to his grandson's question,

> "The rays of sun are very sharp,
> But the rays that shine from this one son
> Cool your body when they touch you.
> This is surely the light of a mighty one."

Then Arana and Agnidattapura went to Kapilavastu, where they said,

> "Great King, we have traveled here
> To seek a viewing of your son.
> To seek one sight of this mighty one,
> A chief, a leader in the world."

The Bodhisattva was sleeping, yet he beheld these two sages. The sages said,

> "The well-bred horse
> Sleeps but a quarter night.
> For those with great purpose,
> Sleep lingers not upon the eyes."

And the Bodhisattva's father said to them, "Soothsayers, there is a prophecy that he will become a wheel-turning king. How will this come about?"

Arana said,

> "Oh Lord, the pundits are mistaken.
> In strife-filled times no monarch comes.
> This source of Dharma and great virtue
> Will conquer sleep, and awaken."

THE THIRD SAGE'S PREDICTION

The *Scripture on Recalling the Buddha* tells the story differently: The king and the queen took the prince to see Kala the sage so that he might interpret the signs. Kala beheld a right-spinning conch shell in the middle of the Bodhisattva's brow. Kala then took hold of the tuft of hair extending from the Bodhisattva's head in order to measure it. It was fifteen finger-widths in height, and was the color of blue beryl. As soon as Kala let the tuft go, it also began spinning to the right. The tuft transformed into a crystalline ball, erupting with light rays of a million colors.

Now, Shakyamuni's father, the king, said to the Bodhisattva,

"The sages offer prayers to you.
The whole world offers its prayers too,
I as well prostrate to you."

And the king prostrated at the feet of the Bodhisattva.

PRAISE FROM THE FAMILY GODS

Now, the citizens of Kapilavastu took the Bodhisattva to the temple of their family gods. The Bodhisattva tried to tell them that there was no need to go there, but they did not hear him. So as soon as he set his right foot upon the doorstep the earth rumbled. All the statues within the temple, the gods Brahma, Indra, Vishnu, Vaishravana, and the rest rose up from their places and prostrated at the Bodhisattva's feet.

These stories give just the merest hint of the wonders that the Bodhisattva performed at the time of his birth. To recount them fully would simply take forever! So I have only included the quintessence of his acts.

As the *Praise in One Hundred and Fifty Verses* says,

Who has so many qualities,
Who has no equal in his strength,
Whose wondrous acts are without end,
To you, self-made, I fold my hands in prayer.

The Ornament for the Thousand-Light Eon, the Life Story of Lord Victor Shakyamuni.

Act Three.

How he was born.

CHAPTER FOUR

EDUCATION

The essence of existence in all time,
Moon, bright and clear in your heart,
Such wonders—the radiance of your good karma—
Light up the sky without end.

IN SCHOOL

The Bodhisattva was quite famous among all the kingdoms throughout the land. Yet it was his way to live in accord with the world. So, along with the ten thousand other children of the Shakya family, the young prince attended the classes of the language tutor Vishvamitra.

"Good teacher, which scripts will you teach me?" asked Shakyamuni. "The Brahmi script? Karoshti? The Lotus Heart script?"

And he listed every kind of script, sixty-four in all.

"Master, which of the sixty-four scripts will you teach me?"

Vishvamitra was astounded. A smile spread across his face as he said,

"This person is quite wonderful!
He's learned all scholarship, and yet
He follows worldly ways, and so
He has come to grammar school.

Scripts even the name of which
I have never known myself,
Even though he knows these well,
He has come to school to learn."

At this very moment thirty-two thousand people were brought to complete enlightenment. And this is the reason that the Bodhisattva entered grammar school.

THE SHADOW

Once, the Bodhisattva went into the gardens. There he sat in the shade of a Jambu tree, and meditated within all four forms of concentration. At just this time, five magicians were flying through the sky, making their way from the south to the north. These five sages were of another religious tradition. But the brilliance radiated by the Bodhisattva as he meditated stopped them in their path. They fell to the ground next to him, and bowed down to him. Then they praised the Bodhisattva.

"He comes as a great sea to cool
The pains of affliction's fire in the world.
He will eventually attain
The teaching that fulfills the world."

Now, the shadows of the other trees moved to the west, while the shadow of that Jambu tree did not move from the Bodhisattva's body.

The king witnessed this miracle and said,

"At the time that you were born,
And as you sit in radiant trance,

Leader, these are two such times,
Protector, that I must pray at your feet."

The Bodhisattva attended school to study the subjects
studied by people of the world: grammar, mathematics,
the arts, archery, and more. He studied with Vishvamitra, Arjuna, his uncle Sahadeva, and a host of other in-
structors.

In each and every subject the Bodhisattva was able to
teach his teachers more than they were able to teach him.

*The Ornament for the Thousand-Light Eon, the Life Story
of Lord Victor Shakyamuni.*

Act Four.

Education in the arts.

CHAPTER FIVE

HAREM

Desire's five arrows, a youthful glance,
These cannot pierce your heart.
By custom of old kings and queens you stay,
To enlighten every single living person.

THE SEARCH FOR A BRIDE

Now, the elders of the Shakya family came before King Suddhodana.

"Lord, the diviners predict that if this young one were to marry, he would become a wheel-turning king," they said. "We must search for a queen."

"Find out where there is a girl who will be suitable for this boy!" said the king.

Five hundred members of the Shakya family came forward.

"Our daughter is suitable!" each one of them said.

"We must go and ask the boy himself," said the king. So they questioned the Bodhisattva.

"I will give you an answer within seven days," he said. And yet he thought,

"Its faults are quite well-known to me, desire,
The root of suffering, fighting, jealousy.

It terrifies me like a poison leaf,
Like fire or the slashing of a sword.

I do not long for objects of desire.
It is not right for me to cavort with women,
Calm of mind, with bliss from concentration,
I shall live in the forest without speaking."

This is what he thought. And yet he was both astute and compassionate, so he also considered:

"The lotus blooms within the muddy pool,
The king is worshipped among commoners.
And when the Bodhisattva gains a supreme crowd,
He leads ten million people beyond death.

Learned bodhisattvas came before me.
All taught through wives and sons and servants,
Not controlled by lust, good thoughts not rent apart.
So shall I teach according to their ways."

And so he listed the good qualities of a woman in a letter.
"If there is a woman like this," he said, "please offer her to me."
Then the king called for his minister, a brahmin.
"Bring me a woman who has all of these qualities!"
And this brahmin traveled throughout the lands. At last he came upon Gopa, the daughter of Shakya Dandapani. He presented the Bodhisattva's letter to her. She smiled, saying,

"Brahmin, these qualities I do possess,
A man of character may marry me.
Should this youth so wish, let him not tarry,
How can he take a woman of low birth?"

The minister related this to the king, who said,

> "These women are great liars, trust them not!
> In seven days bring all women to meet,
> The Boy will give them presents. He'll decide!"

On the seventh day the young Bodhisattva went to the reception hall. He offered presents to many becoming girls. Yet, as they were unable to bear his brilliance, they soon departed.

At last Gopa came before him. But all of the gifts had already been given away.

"Have I offended you in some way?" Gopa cast a smile at him. "Do you despise me?"

"No, you have not offended me," said the prince. "It is just . . . You have come too late!"

And he gave her a ring worth one hundred thousand pieces of gold. Gopa took the ring and returned home.

Now, the king's spies had overheard their conversation.

"Shakyamuni set eyes upon young Gopa," they informed the king. "And they even talked briefly!"

THE TOURNAMENT

Presently the king sent a messenger to Gopa's father, Shakya Dandapani.

"Give your daughter to the prince!" ordered the king.

"The prince was born into a life of ease within the palace," replied Dandapani. "He does not know any martial arts. According to the customs of my clan, I may only give my daughter to one who knows the martial arts. I may not give her to one who knows nothing of such things!"

News of this was related to the king,

"Twice now have I been offended over this!" he thought.

When young Shakyamuni heard about this, he went to the king.

"Is it not proper that you tell me what is wrong?" asked Shakyamuni.

The king related the matter to him, and young Shakyamuni agreed to a contest in the martial arts. The king was delighted. He proclaimed that there would be a tournament in the martial arts.

Seven days later, five hundred young Shakya men and an innumerable crowd of gods and humans assembled. Gopa was offered up as the prize to be given to the winner.

"Whoever is victorious in swordsmanship, archery, wrestling, and the like will win her!" promised the king.

Now, Devadatta came forth first. Full of envy and pride, he walked up to an elephant as it was led in and killed it by merely striking it once with his palm.

Then Sundarananda came forth.

"Who killed this elephant?" he asked.

"Devadatta did!"

So Sundarananda hoisted up the dead elephant and cast it just beyond the city gates.

Now, the Bodhisattva came forth. He picked the elephant up by its big toe, and hurled it a full league beyond the seven walls and the seven moats of the city. A great trench formed where the elephant landed, and this became famous as the Elephant Trench.

The Bodhisattva was also the winner in writing, mathematics, the long jump, swimming, and running.

Now, Shakyamuni's brothers Nanda and Ananda both stepped forward to pit their strength against Shakyamuni. Yet no sooner than his hand had touched them, they fell down. Devadatta came at him, but the Bodhisattva picked him up with his right hand, spun him around in the air, and slammed him into the ground. And though he did this, he did not harm Devadatta.

All the young men of the Shakya family attacked him now, but the Bodhisattva had only to touch them and they each fell to the ground.

Next they held the archery contest. An iron drum was set up as a target. Ananda shot his arrow from a distance of two miles. Devadatta shot from a distance of four miles. Sundarananda shot from six miles. Shakya Dandapani shot from a distance of two leagues. Each arrow pierced the iron drum and struck the ground beyond. But none went farther than this.

Then the Bodhisattva had the iron drum placed at a distance of ten miles. He had seven trees arranged in a row behind the iron drum, and beyond the trees he had an iron boar placed. From the temple he brought out Lion Jaw, the bow that had belonged to his grandfather. He strung the bow and shot his arrow. The arrow pierced the iron drum. It pierced the seven trees. It pierced the iron boar. Finally it pierced the earth and disappeared.

The place where the well-like hole appeared is known as the Arrow Well.

Next the Bodhisattva proved superior in palm reading, elephant riding, even incense making. And he proved superior in every other art in this world and beyond as well.

GOPA THE PRINCESS

At last, Shakya Dandapani offered his daughter Gopa to Siddhartha.

The Bodhisattva acted according to the customs of this world. He anointed Gopa supreme among eighty-four thousand young women. Then he let it appear as if he enjoyed frolicking with them.

Then several bodhisattvas, gods, and serpents considered the following. "If the Holy One remains long in the company of his princesses, living beings who are ready to receive his teachings will cease to exist. If this happens, he may not undertake renunciation."

The gods had faith in him. "He must undertake renunciation," they resolved. "He must achieve awakening and teach the Dharma."

The Ornament for the Thousand-Light Eon, the Life Story of Lord Victor Shakyamuni.

Act Five.

Pleasant diversions with the harem.

CHAPTER SIX

RENUNCIATION

For people in this unforgiving world,
Wrought of iron, forged from diamond core,
You took renunciation and with skill,
You turned the kingdom down. To you I pray.

SONG OF THE GODS

Now, by the age of seventeen the Bodhisattva had shown himself to be supreme in all of the arts. And up until the age of twenty-nine he appeared to bask in the glories of the kingdom.

Presently the Buddhas encouraged him with soothing verses:

"You once beheld the hundred human ills,
You said, 'I will become their protector,
Their refuge, source and shelter, friend and aid!'
Such was the prayer you made once, long ago.

Remember now your prayer to help humans,
Your hero's deeds and virtue long ago.
This is your time, the hour for you is now.
Great Sage, you must renounce your home for good!"

He also heard encouraging words wafting from the music performed by his harem. The music told of the lives he had lived before, and then it sang:

> "The pain of age and illness burns the worlds.
> With no protector, people never know
> How to depart this blazing fire of death.
> They scramble like a bee inside a jar.
>
> Autumn clouds, the three worlds pass fleeting.
> We're born, we die, we're actors on a stage.
> One life, a lightning flash across the sky.
> A cascade falling, speeding down the cliff."

Three million two hundred gods encouraged him as well. They said,

> "A voice so sweet, a voice so soft
> Must heed Dipankara's prophecy.
> Fulfill its perfect truth without mistake,
> Proclaim the Victor's Words, we ask you now."

Now, the king had a dream in which the Bodhisattva renounced the kingdom. When he awoke, he went to question the Bodhisattva.

"Is this so?" asked the king.

"It is so," said the Bodhisattva.

"This is a sign that the Bodhisattva will undertake renunciation," thought the king.

The king had three palaces built so that the Bodhisattva would remain attached to the kingdom: a cool palace for spring, one just right for summer, and a warm one for winter. Five hundred men were stationed along every staircase to each of the palaces. When the Bodhisattva descended, they spread the word for half a mile.

"The prince may not move about unguarded!" said the king.

CHANDAKA THE CHARIOTEER

"The Bodhisattva will depart through the royal gates." This was the prophecy made by all the diviners.

So the king had massive bolts made for the royal gates. Five hundred men were needed to push back these bolts. Any request to open the gates was required to be issued from half a mile away.

Then the Bodhisattva called Chandaka, his charioteer. "Prepare a chariot so that I may go to the royal gardens."

Chandaka related this to the king.

"Nothing that is displeasing to the prince should be visible," said the king. "Everything should be pleasant!"

And yet the Bodhisattva left through the Eastern Gate. He beheld a man afflicted with the pains of aging. This man was in fact an emanation produced by the gods through the power of the Bodhisattva himself.

He asked Chandaka,

> "Charioteer, this man is weak and slight,
> His flesh and blood withered, his skin wrinkled,
> White hair, lost teeth, and body very frail,
> He walks in pain upon a staff—who is he?"

Chandaka replied,

> "My only god, this man is beat by age,
> His strength and senses lost, he suffers now."

Chandaka answered all of the Bodhisattva's questions about this and other matters. And the Bodhisattva said,

"I must go back, do turn this chariot quick.
If even I will age, what use is play?"

And they returned to the palace.

In the same way the Bodhisattva went out through the Southern Gate. There he saw a sick person.

He went out once more, this time through the Western Gate. There he saw a dead person. And again he asked Chandaka who this person was. Chandaka told him about death, and the Bodhisattva said,

"If only age and death would disappear!
If pain is great bound in this five-heaped self,
What need to speak of age, death ever present?
Go back, I must seek means to be free of this!"

Then they returned to the palace.

Once more they went out, this time through the Northern Gate, where the Bodhisattva saw a mendicant. And even though he knew full well, he asked Chandaka once again.

"Who is this person in saffron robes?" he asked—even though he well knew. "His appearance is so peaceful and gentle."

"This is a renunciant," said Chandaka. "He is seeking complete peace, free of all attachment."

The Bodhisattva said,

"This you describe I now desire as well.
Renunciation, long praised by the wise,
This now brings benefit to me and others.
It results in immortal bliss and ease."

King Suddhodana witnessed all of this as well, and he tried to insulate the Bodhisattva. He ordered the construction of another wall. He ordered another moat. He ordered more locks for the palace gates. He posted guards at the crossroads around the city. He ordered the harem to perform songs and dramas.

OMENS OF THE DEPARTURE

During all of this there were many omens that the Bodhisattva would depart. The birds did not sing. The lotuses withered. The trees bore no fruit. The flutes and lutes did not make music. When the drums were struck, they would make no sound. Gopa had dreams of earthquakes and other omens. And because of this the king knew that the departure was a reality in the depths of the Bodhisattva's heart.

And the Bodhisattva dreamed as well:

He stirred the ocean with his legs. The earth was his bed, Mount Meru his pillow. Light broke through the darkness, and a parasol rose up out of the earth and covered the three worlds. Four black-and-white beasts and four multicolored birds appeared, and then became a single color. The Bodhisattva climbed a mountain of vomit, yet even as he did so he did not become soiled. He rescued people who were being carried away by the waters. He healed those who were sick. At last he sat down upon a lion throne at the peak of Mount Meru while the gods paid homage to him.

"It would not be right," thought the Bodhisattva, "if I were to depart without being granted leave by my father." So he went to make his request.

"The time has come for me to undertake renunciation," he said. "Please do not forbid this or be unhappy."

"I will give you the best of whatever you could possibly wish for," said the king, "if only you will remain in the palace!"

"Then give me the best!" said the Bodhisattva.

"No aging.

"No sickness.

"No death.

"No decay."

"I do not have the power to give these," said the king.

The Bodhisattva politely made his request a second time, and then a third time.

In the end, his father consented.

"I am glad that you will benefit others and put an end to rebirth," he said. "May you fulfill your wishes."

Yet despite this the king initiated still more measures throughout the palace to detain the Bodhisattva.

THE GODS INTERVENE

Now, the guardian deities, including the five hundred sons of Hariti, the magnificent four kings, and the Thirty-Three Gods, pondered the Bodhisattva.

"The Bodhisattva is ready to leave."

"If we work hard to make offerings to him, it will happen."

The Bodhisattva at once became conscious of the four vows he had made long ago. He looked out upon his harem. Dharmacarin and other heavenly sons had transformed the harem into a grotesque spectacle, and a feeling came over the Bodhisattva. He was living in a cemetery!

> "Oh, how all of these creatures suffer so!
> Where is there joy amidst a demon horde?
> They grasp what they desire as if it's real."

And as he said these words he contemplated the hideousness of the harem.

Then the Bodhisattva went to the roof of his mansion. He prayed to all the Buddhas in every direction, and when he looked around he saw that Indra, the four kings, as well as the sun and the moon were also praying. When he saw that the star Pushpa was on the rise, he said to Chandaka,

> "Good fortune this is! I will attain my goals.
> Tonight, without a doubt, I will succeed.
> Chandaka, quick, right now, do not delay,
> Dress the king of horses, bring him to me,
> I now go to the forest, where sages delight."

In sadness Chandaka listened to his words.

"God, midnight is a time of terrible things! This is not a good time to travel into the gardens or the forests," he begged the Bodhisattva.

But the Bodhisattva said,

> "I seek the welfare of all living beings,
> To gain awakening, free of age and death.
> Long ago I vowed to free the world,
> And now the time has come to keep that pledge."

The Bodhisattva spoke at length of the faults of desire. And when he had finished speaking, Chandaka dressed Kantaka the horse and brought him to the Bodhisattva.

THE DEPARTURE

Then four sons of the gods lifted Kantaka into the air. Indra opened the palace gate, and the four guardian kings and their troops protected the Bodhisattva.

Brahma and the other gods prayed to him, and the Bodhisattva departed the palace.

He passed right by the royal guard station. He traveled all the way to the foot of the Immaculate Shrine. And there he gave Kantaka and all of his jewelry to Chandaka.

> "Until I've reached the supreme path
> That's taught by all awakened ones,
> I will not set foot on the ground
> Of Kapilavastu, my home."

Saddened, Chandaka took Kantaka and the jewelry and left. And at this place a shrine was made, and it was called Chandaka's Return.

At the foot of the Immaculate Shrine, the Bodhisattva cut his hair. He used a knife made of sandalwood that was the color of the blue utpala flower. The gods took his hair away and created a shrine for it. This shrine became known as the Topknot Shrine.

"My fine clothing of Varanasi linen is not in keeping with the life of renunciation," thought the Bodhisattva. "I must find some clothing that is appropriate."

Then a god from one of the pure lands appeared in the form of a hunter and offered a saffron robe to the Bodhisattva. The Bodhisattva gave the Varanasi linen to the god, who received it with both hands and raised it to the top of his head in praise. Then the god returned to the land of the gods. Before he left, Chandaka witnessed all of this, and built a shrine there. This became known as the Shrine of the Saffron Robe Reception.

By now the news had spread all the way to heaven. "Siddhartha has become a renunciant!" Chandaka returned with the Bodhisattva's horse and jewelry, and informed the king and the princess of the terrible news. The Bodhisattva's horse, Kantaka, fell ill at this time, and in the end passed away—according to the *Scripture on the Departure*.

After the Bodhisattva cut off his topknot he became a renunciant. Now, he traveled to the place where the brahmin teacher Raivata stayed. Next he went to Vaishali, where Arada Kalama was teaching the perceptual sphere of nonexistence to three hundred disciples. The Bodhisattva went before Arada Kalama and became his disciple. He studied the teachings of Arada Kalama and he achieved results.

"And yet," he thought, "no certainty will come from this practice."

So he went to study the peak experience among the seven hundred disciples of Udraka Ramaputra.

"This too will not lead to liberation from suffering," he thought.

And he became dissatisfied with the teaching and left Udraka Ramaputra.

He eventually traveled to Magadha. He went to Mount Pandava and the Tadopa Gate, and then came to the city of Rajagriha. The people of the city looked upon him with great devotion.

King Bimbisara also had faith in the Bodhisattva. The king even offered the kingdom to him, but the Bodhisattva had no wish for a kingdom.

The Ornament for the Thousand-Light Eon, the Life Story of Lord Victor Shakyamuni.

Act Six.

How the Bodhisattva renounced the kingdom and took ordination by himself.

CHAPTER SEVEN

AUSTERITY

In Akanishta Heaven, body and mind fully developed,
In front of Buddhas as numerous as a heap of sesame seeds,
You are blessed and now named Vajradhatu,
You are awakening again—to you I bow.

THREE METAPHORS

The Bodhisattva remained with five ascetics, and together they undertook renunciation at the top of Mount Gaya. While they lived there the Bodhisattva had a flash of insight and developed three metaphors for the experience of awakening that no one had heard before:

A piece of driftwood that is soaking wet will not catch fire no matter how much it is rubbed. Just so, the body and the mind that are dowsed in desire are unable to reach liberation.

Even if the driftwood is only moist this will still be the case. Just so, even if the body is kept apart from desire, if the mind is not kept apart, one remains unable to reach liberation.

Only a dry stick is able to catch fire. Just so, body and mind must be well separated from desire.

Given this, the Bodhisattva came to understand that cognition, vision, and perception were needed, and that the styles of asceticism followed in these degenerate times were unhelpful. A reformer needed to refute these practices.

"So," he thought, "I must begin to practice asceticism and austerity."

PRACTICES OF AUSTERITY

The Bodhisattva walked to the banks of the Nairanjana River. For six years he remained in Sky Concentration. He lived on a single sesame seed, a single jujube, and a single grain of rice. For six years he practiced such austerity. The Bodhisattva learned to suspend his breath yet remain alive:

Sitting in a meditation position upon unswept ground, he clenched his teeth and pressed his tongue to his palate. He mentally grasped and bound his mind. Yet when he did so, a stream of particles streamed from his barely open mouth and dripped onto the ground. It felt as though a strong person was crushing his neck. Despite these intense sensations, he did not become discouraged.

Now, when the Bodhisattva had entered the Sky Concentration and suspended his respiration, all of his vital winds collected at the crown of his skull. This caused unbearably sharp pains in his head. It was as if he was being stabbed with iron daggers. A loud intense sound emitted from his ears as well.

As this was happening, the sons of the gods came before the Bodhisattva's mother, Goddess Mahamaya.

"Your son has died!" they said.

The goddess went to the Bodhisattva, and beheld him. His body was emaciated. He looked like death.

"As soon as you were born," Mahamaya lamented, "you made a vow: 'This will be my final life.' Now, your vow is incomplete! The prophecy of Kala the Sage is not true at all!"

The Bodhisattva replied,

> "Sun and moon and stars may fall to earth,
> But as a common man I will not die.
> So you should not feel suffering at this,
> For soon, you see, I awake as a Buddha."

And as he said this Mahamaya became joyful and returned to her world.

Now, the Bodhisattva's limbs were like the branches of the Asita or Kalika trees, barren of foliage. His scalp was as shriveled as an old gourd. His eyes sunk into their sockets, like a star down a well. His ribs were sticking out, and his spine looked like a braid of hair. When he tried to rise, he fell on his face; when he tried to sit down, he collapsed on his back. Even the hairs on his body had withered or had fallen out. Whatever was good about his appearance had faded away.

The ghosts living in the surrounding villages saw him.

"Alas, the ascetic Gautama is blackened!" they said. "Alas, the ascetic Gautama has turned blue!"

In this way the Bodhisattva practiced austerities for six years without rising from his cross-legged position. And even though he did so, he did not reduce his negative mental states. It did not appear that he would achieve unsurpassed enlightenment through either the embrace of the sense pleasures nor the endurance of pain. And so, motivated by compassion for the people of the future, the Bodhisattva took some humble food.

His five companions considered this:

"If he was unable to achieve enlightenment through any sort of ascetic practice," they said, "he will not be able to attain enlightenment at all now!"

Then the five sages fell out with him and went to Deer Park.

After this the Bodhisattva found the funeral wrappings of a woman named Radha, who had been servant to Sujata. The gods dug out a pond with their own hands, and Indra placed a stone by the pond. There the Bodhisattva washed the wrappings.

The work fatigued him. He thought to rise up from the pond, but as he tried to rise the demon Mara conjured high cliffs around the pond. Just in time a tree goddess lowered a branch down to him. He grasped the branch and emerged from the pond. At the foot of this Kakubha tree he sewed the remains of the wrappings into a monk's garment. The Pure Land gods offered a saffron robe to him. He accepted the robe and walked to a nearby village.

Another scripture says that as the Bodhisattva practiced austerities, the Transcendent Ones caught his attention by snapping their fingers and roused him from his motionless concentration. The village woman Sujata then offered him a meal made from the best milk and honey. He ate this, and his former golden complexion was restored.

An esoteric scripture says that the Bodhisattva left his maturing physical body here on earth while he traveled in his wisdom body to a celestial palace in heaven. Amid an assembly of Transcendent Ones as numerous as the sesame seeds in a giant heap, the Bodhisattva attained the empowerment of Vajradhatu, and achieved perfect enlightenment. Only then did he return to his maturing physical body to act as if he was achieving enlightenment.

Because of this the Buddha says,

> "Where perfect Buddhas dwell, Buddhas awake.
> One incarnation, here I become a Buddha."

———

The Ornament for the Thousand-Light Eon, the Life Story of Lord Victor Shakyamuni.

Act Seven.

How the Bodhisattva practiced austerities for six years on the banks of the River Nairanjana.

CHAPTER EIGHT

THE DIAMOND THRONE

At first you vowed to gain enlightenment,
Over three countless eons you honed skills.
Then you vanquished far the demon's hordes.
You gained enlightenment—to you I bow.

SUJATA'S GIFT

Now, Indra summoned the village woman Sujata. She skimmed the milk of one thousand cows seven times, mixed fresh rice and grain into the cream, and boiled it. Within this mixture the endless knot and other good-luck signs clearly appeared, filling Sujata with joy. Because of these signs, her soothsayer predicted that she would achieve the nectar of immortality.

Then Sujata filled a golden bowl with the honey cream and offered it to the Bodhisattva. He accepted this gift and walked to the banks of the Nairanjana River. He set down his food and religious robes on the bank and began to bathe. And as he did so the gods made proper offerings to him.

The gods returned to take the water remaining after the Bodhisattva bathed. Sujata even took the shavings of his hair and his beard.

Then the Bodhisattva ate the porridge that Sujata had given him. And as he finished eating it, his body took on the color of refined gold. He looked at his appearance but remained unsatisfied. The river serpents offered a lion-base throne to him, and he sat down upon it. He then cast the golden bowl into the river, and the serpent king Sagara grabbed for it. But Indra appeared in the form of a bird, swept down, and took the bowl to the Thirty-Three Gods' Heaven. Every year the gods hold a feast in honor of this bowl.

JOURNEY TO THE DIAMOND THRONE

The Bodhisattva had bathed and he had taken food. Now, his body was strong. With the strength of a super-man, it was now time for him to vanquish the demon Mara at the foot of the Bodhi tree.

The Bodhisattva considered his route to the Diamond Throne, the Heart of Enlightenment. And as he did so, the wind and the rain swept clear a path and settled the dust with a sprinkling of water. All of the hills and the trees, and every newborn child as well—all bowed their heads in the direction of the Heart of Enlightenment.

Even powerful Brahma, Lord of the Universe, looked on. "Pay your respects," he said to all who were gathered around him, "for tonight the Bodhisattva will arrive at the Heart of Enlightenment!" And so offerings beyond thought miraculously appeared before the Bodhisattva.

And now the Bodhisattva's body emitted countless rays of light. They covered the entire world in luminescence, and purified people so that they would be worthy recipients for his teaching. The serpent king Kalika witnessed this, and knew that the Bodhisattva would soon become a Buddha. He praised him with poetry.

The Bodhisattva traveled to the Heart of Enlightenment.

And as he arrived to sit down there, he assumed a physical form that disciples would be capable of understanding. He donned the appearance that was appropriate for the common disciples of this world.

A grass cutter named Svastika sat with a bundle of grass on the right side of the path.

The Bodhisattva said,

> "Oh, Svastika, please, quick, give me some grass.
> Today this grass will serve great ends for me.
> For I will vanquish the demon and his hordes.
> And gain the holy peace, enlightenment."

Svastika offered beautiful fresh green grass to the Bodhisattva, and he carried it to the Heart of Enlightenment.

Now, at the Heart of Enlightenment a thousand Bodhi trees sprang forth, and a thousand lion-base thrones. The Bodhisattva circled the third tree four times. Then he set his grass down at its base, with the grass tips facing inward and the roots facing outward. He sat down facing the east and settled his body in a straight and firm posture.

Then the Bodhisattva appeared to make this vow:

> "My body may wither upon this seat—okay.
> My skin, my bones, my flesh may all decay.
> Yet, until I gain hard-won enlightenment,
> I will not move this body from its seat."

Even the gods had a vision that this tree was for them a wish-granting tree. And because they beheld the tree in this way, countless brilliant and sparkling gifts appeared under the fantastic Bodhi tree, treasures for the gods.

The boundless excellent features of the Bodhi tree appeared as a palace. Bodhisattvas from every direction were seated within this palace. The world and all its unfathomable seas appeared as a limitless Buddha realm. And even if one had endless eons to describe the vastness of the palace and its inhabitants, one would not behold their limit.

And every last detail of this was created by the Bodhisattva's previous vow to achieve enlightenment.

The Ornament for the Thousand-Light Eon, the Life Story of Lord Victor Shakyamuni.

Act Eight.

Journey to the Diamond Throne, the Heart of Enlightenment.

CHAPTER NINE

DEMONS

Cheerfully dwelling amid the fires of hell,
One hundred eons for every single life!
Even among all loving, kindly people,
You shine, a real diamond in a sea of counterfeits.

"It is evening now," thought the Bodhisattva.

"But I have yet to conquer the demon Mara. Until I do so it is not right that I attain enlightenment."

And so the Bodhisattva cast forth a brilliant light from the space between his eyes. Destroyer of the Demon's Realm—this was the name of the light. And this light threw the entire universe into bold relief.

Words sounded from the light, and wicked Mara heard them:

"That noble being, who labored many eons,
Suddhodana's son, who gave up the kingdom,
Who truly hopes to save all living beings,
Has come before the tree today. Beware!"

After this wicked Mara had thirty-two nightmares. And because of these he amassed a demon army of ten battalions. Then he spoke to the Bodhisattva in a terrifying voice:

"Tormentors, ghouls, and serpent shapes,
Blood drinkers, flesh eaters, ghostly forms,
Lowly, ugly, ferocious sorts,
This trickster demon conjures all.

Mountains circle in from all directions,
Boulders, weapons rain down from the sky,
Blazing daggers fall down on you now.
Son of a Shakya, you will be ground to dust!"

Yet the Bodhisattva said,

"The king of the Shakya knows reality,
To form as a matrix with no fixed core.
As vast as heaven is his mind, and so,
He does not fear these troops, these crafty tricks."

The Bodhisattva did not have even a hint of lingering fear. On the contrary, he was full of compassion. And because of this the weapons hurled at him by the opposing side all transformed into flowers as they rained down upon him.

Because of this wicked Mara slandered the Bodhisattva as he paced:

"Endless sacrifice I've made before!
If you had done so, you would have a witness,
But you have no witness now, and so,
Although you make these claims, you have no proof!"

The Bodhisattva placed his right hand upon the ground and said,

"This earth is witness for all living beings,
It is impartial toward all existence.

The earth shall be my witness, I do not lie.
You, Earth, I call you as my witness here!"

The ground trembled, and Sthavara, goddess of the earth, emerged halfway out of the soil. She folded her hands in reverence to the Bodhisattva.

"Great One, it is so," she said. "It is just as you have declared. The truth of this is evident to me. And yet, Lord, now you have become the witness for the world and the gods."

They heard these words, wicked Mara and his troops.
Like foxes at the lion's roar through trees,
Like black crows as the rock is hurled at them,
They panicked in their hearts, and all then fled.

And the Lord of Desire retreated to a place of mourning.

Now, Shri and seven other forest goddesses lavished sixteen types of praise upon the Bodhisattva.

"You are as beautiful as the waxing moon!" they said.

And the Pure Land gods insulted the demon Mara in sixteen different ways.

"You are as weak as an old bull stuck in a swamp!" they said.

The gods attempted to push wicked Mara back, but he would not be repelled. He hurled all kinds of weapons at the Bodhisattva, and conjured many illusions. And still he was unable to gain the upper hand. His demon hordes were dispersed. He was not able to reunite them for seven days, and during this time many demons developed an enlightened attitude.

Now, Tanha, Arati, and the rest of the demon Mara's daughters witnessed their father in his place of mourning. Once again they tried to stop the Bodhisattva, this time by appealing to his desires and seducing him. But they were transformed through the power of the Bodhisatt-va's blessing into old and sickly women. The Bodhisattva also had the power to protect them from this, and when the daughters praised him they transformed back into their original forms.

With skillful means such as this the Bodhisattva brought three hundred twenty million demons to enlight-enment. During these events the Bodhisattva performed other magical feats, such as placing all of the people of the world into a magnificent diamond tent when they were under threat of being turned to dust. But these are explained elsewhere.

The Ornament for the Thousand-Light Eon, the Life Story of Lord Victor Shakyamuni.

Act Nine.

Vanquishing the demon.

CHAPTER TEN

ENLIGHTENMENT

With diamond concentration you beheld
The wisdom at the end of all our lives.
You labored to stop sowing future deeds,
And reaped a feast of joy! To you I bow.

THE FINAL WATCH

The Bodhisattva had defeated the entire army of the demon Mara. Now, in the first watch of the night, he worked through the four stages of concentration and the three types of understanding. Then came the final watch of the night.

Just before dawn, in an instant, in the single beat of a drum, the Bodhisattva understood.

He understood the twelve links of dependent arising. He understood the four noble truths. And because of this instantaneous understanding he became truly enlightened.

And in an instant he grew to a height of seven palm trees.

"My path has come to an end," he said. "My suffering has been pacified."

The gods offered flowers, scattering so many that he was covered up to his knees. The world was bathed in light. The ground shook. Buddhas from every direction showed their delight and extended their hands in salutation to him.

"Just as we achieved enlightenment, so you have become a Buddha," they said, "just like butter and butter cream."

The daughters of the gods praised him as well. And then the Teacher also spoke:

"Virtue brings bliss, it removes every pain,
The virtuous person's goal is always achieved.
The demon vanquished, I quickly reached awakening.
I won release from suffering, peaceful, cool.
Whoever practices virtue finds content."

From that moment he undertook the endless enjoyments of the Buddhas, and these could not be described even if one had an eon in which to try.

SEVEN WEEKS

Now, for the first week after the Enlightenment the Buddha was nurtured by the joy of enlightenment at the incredible door of contemplative concentration. This was now his true nature.

At the heart of the earth, where
The Buddhas with ten powers pray and are blessed,
The lotus-seat posture of the Victor
Will not fail for seven days.

During the second week the Buddha rose from his seat and traversed the length of the three thousand worlds. He also taught the *Scripture of the Ten Grounds, The Vast Array of the Buddha,* and *The Design of Samantabhadra's Realm* in the company of Vajragarbha and innumerable other bodhisattvas at a temple in the celestial realm of the gods who control the emanations of others.

Next came the third week. "In this place I have achieved true and complete buddhahood," thought the Transcendent One. "I have reached the end of beginningless birth, aging, and death." And with his eyes wide open he beheld the Heart of Enlightenment. He also taught many esoteric scriptures during the third week, including the *All-Conquering Wrathful Vajra*, the *Noble Tara Scripture*, and secret spell scriptures for Mahakala, Shridevi, and other defenders of the faith. Their origins are told in the prefaces to their respective esoteric scriptures.

During the fourth week the Transcendent One traveled from the eastern sea to the western sea.

Now, wicked Mara came before the Transcendent One.

"Lord, is it not time for you to pass into final nirvana?" he said. "Bliss-Gone One, I beseech you to completely pass from suffering."

"Wicked One, until my monks are famed as disciplined elders, until the words 'Buddha,' 'Dharma,' and 'Sangha' are firmly established in the world, until a great many bodhisattvas are destined to achieve complete enlightenment, I will not completely pass from suffering," said the Buddha.

Wicked Mara was despondent and unhappily went off in one direction. With head hung low, he scratched out doodles in the dirt.

"The Buddha is now beyond my grasp," thought wicked Mara.

When the fifth week came around, a terrible storm rose up for seven days, and the Transcendent One stayed in the house of the serpent king Mucilinda. All the serpent kings gathered together and continually covered the body of the Lord with their hoods to protect him from the cold. After one week had passed the serpents knew that the storm was over. They unwrapped themselves from the Buddha's body, prayed to his feet with their heads, and returned to their own realms.

During the sixth week the Buddha uttered this verse to the ascetics at the foot of the Nyagrodha tree:

> "One who hears and sees the faith finds joy.
> One in joyful solitude finds bliss.
> Whoever subdues beings without harm
> Brings a blissful joy to all the world."

The Buddha also stayed in the Sala Cave performing miracles. While he stayed here Indra Kaushika died and fell into rebirth as an animal. He was terrified! The Buddha came before him with eighty-four thousand sons of the gods and gave a teaching to Indra on prolonging life. Today this is known as the Rite of the Four Hundred. He also gave many teachings from all three vehicles—Hinayana, Mahayana, and Vajrayana—at this time.

During the seventh week the Transcendent One was seated at the foot of a fig tree when two merchants, Trapusha and Bhallika, offered him food.

"The Buddhas of the past gave up bowls made of silver and gold," thought the Buddha. "It would be in keeping with monastic practice were I to accept this food in a stone bowl."

The four guardian kings knew what he was thinking, and each one offered him a stone bowl.

"This is not good," the Transcendent One thought. "Each one has offered me a bowl. And yet if I accept one, the others will be unhappy! I shall take the four bowls and transform them into a single bowl."

He took the bowls with his right hand, and spoke to the guardian king Vaishravana.

> "You give a bowl to a Transcendent One,
> And you become a vessel for the path.
> You give bowls to a person such as me,
> And you never lose your memory or your wits."

He gave a similar verse to each of the other four guardian kings, and transformed their four bowls into a single bowl.

The merchants Trapusha and Bhalika then offered the food to him and in turn the Buddha praised them.

> "You who work the gods' blessing,
> Who bring blessings to every quarter
> Your noble aims will be fulfilled,
> And all will be set right for you."

The Buddha gave them many blessings, and he predicted that they would become Buddhas such as Madhisambhava.

So for seven weeks the Buddha turned the wheel of Dharma endlessly. But this is only so from the perspective of the Mahayana, for this is not a part of the Shravaka tradition.

The Ornament for the Thousand-Light Eon, the Life Story of Lord Victor Shakyamuni.

Act Ten.

Enlightenment.

CHAPTER ELEVEN

TEACHING

The tongue that tells of seeking out the ways
Of Buddha bodies and wisdom beyond belief—
The brilliant nature of this Dharma wheel
Brings fortune to the worthy congregation.

"Alas, if this Dharma that I have attained is deep, if it is more than an object of thought, it will be difficult for the people of the world to understand," thought the Lord. "The people here are devotees of Brahma, true. Yet until he asks me directly I will not offer teachings."

"I have attained an essential Dharma,
Simple, peaceful, deep, bright, elemental,
No one I might teach will understand,
So I shall live in silence in the woods."

But then the Buddha lit up the entire world with a magnificent light, and said,

"My love for all the world knows no bounds.
I must not hesitate if others ask me.
All the people here have faith in Brahma,
If he were to ask me, I would teach!"

Now, Crested Brahma came to know something of the Buddha's thoughts.

In an instant Brahma and six million eight hundred thousand other gods folded their hands in reverence for the Transcendent One. Indra called out in friendship three times and prayed to the Buddha.

> "Here in Magadha low teachings reign,
> Corrupt and unholy, poor thinking.
> Open the gate to your essential teaching,
> Please explain your flawless understanding!"

The Transcendent One said,

> "Brahma, people now in Magadha,
> If you can lend an ear and summon faith,
> For all who ever scrutinize this life,
> I will open the gate to vital teachings."

Brahma and the others were overjoyed at his words. Full of faith, they made offerings to him. They sang his praises, and then returned to their own worlds.

The Lord rose up from the foot of the tree at the Heart of Enlightenment. He traveled throughout the billions of worlds in the universe. The last place he traveled to was Magadha. As he wandered around the country, and on the road to Varanasi, he met a beggar who asked him many questions.

The Buddha said,

> "I do not have a master.
> There is no one like me.
> I alone am Buddha,
> Serene and uncorrupted.

To Varanasi I will go,
And coming to that city bright,
For people who are as if blind
I will let forth peerless light."

"May it be so," said the beggar, and he traveled south.

THE FIVE ASCETICS

"To whom should I give these teachings first?" thought the Buddha.

At first he decided to give the teachings to Udraka. But he clairvoyantly saw that Udraka had died seven days ago.

Then he thought to give the teachings to Arada. Yet he too had died three days ago.

"Now, I will teach the five ascetics," he thought, and he left Magadha to travel to Varanasi.

The Buddha traveled north to Mount Gaya, and then on through the cities of Uruvilva, Anala, and Sarathi. Finally he arrived at the banks of the River Ganga, where a boatman demanded a toll for the ferry.

"I have no toll for the ferry," said the Buddha, whereupon he crossed over the river in midair and continued on to the place where the five ascetics were living. King Bimbisara heard about this miracle and forbade the collection of tolls from all renunciants.

Now, the five ascetics saw the Buddha coming from a ways off.

"Lazy mendicant Gautama!" one whispered.

"He eats a lot, and he has fallen from abstinence!"

"None of us should greet him! Don't even get up. Don't give him a robe and bowl. He can just sit here on this leftover seat."

But in his thoughts one ascetic, Kaundinya, did not agree with the others. And as the Buddha approached all five ascetics were overcome by his charisma and they gave up their plan. They rose from their seats. One went to greet him. Another went to fetch water to bathe his feet.

"Welcome!" they said. "Please, would you sit on this cushion?"

The Teacher sat on the cushion and spoke at length to the disciples so that he might boost their faith in him.

"Long-lived Gautama!" they said. "Your senses seem clear. Your skin is totally pure. Have you actually perfected the vision of wisdom?"

"You must not refer to the Transcendent One as 'Long-lived,'" said the Buddha. "Living for a long time brings nothing more than unhappiness. I have attained the essence. I am a Buddha. And I am omniscient; did you not this moment make a secret plan?"

The five ascetics were overcome with shame. They touched the feet of the Buddha, confessed their wrongdoing, and took ordination as monks. They were dressed like householders, so their ordination included an instruction on wearing monastic garments.

THE FIRST TEACHING

Now, the Teacher refreshed himself and wondered where he might begin to turn the wheel of Dharma. He clairvoyantly saw that the previous three Buddhas had turned the wheel of Dharma at Deer Park in Rishipatana on the fourth day of the midsummer month. Then at that very spot one thousand thrones appeared. The Buddha circled the third of these, and at the fourth he sat down with his legs crossed.

The five monks came to him, as did the eight great traditions, and bodhisattvas from every direction. Millions of beings gathered together at Deer Park in style; not a single one of them had even a single hair out of place. Then this great earth rumbled, and light pervaded the three thousand worlds and purified living beings.

Then Brahma touched the feet of the Lord and folded his hands in reverence. The gods offered a wheel made of gold from the river of golden sand. The wheel had one thousand spokes with lavish decorations. Indra, lord of the gods, offered a white conch shell that had belonged to the previous three Buddhas, and begged the Buddha to turn the wheel of Dharma.

Presently several golden deer emerged from the forest. They sat down and set their eyes upon the center of the wheel. Now, all through the first watch of the night the Lord remained in dignified silence. At midnight he gave a sermon to inspire his audience. And in the final watch of the night he called to his five disciples.

"Monks, there are two extremes that a renunciant must not fall into: overindulgence in the pleasures of the senses and self-mortification. You must abandon these two extremes and take up a middle path. This is the teaching of the Transcendent One.

"And this noble path consists of eight components.

"Monks, there are four truths: suffering, the cause of suffering, the removal of suffering, and the path. Suffering must be understood. The cause of suffering must be abandoned . . ."

And he continued up to "Suffering has been completely understood. The cause has been abandoned . . ."

In this way the Buddha recited the four noble truths three times, and thereby turned the wheel of Dharma in its twelve aspects. And through this Kaundinya became an arhat.

With this the Three Jewels were complete.

> Just so, with twelve aspects,
> The Dharma wheel is turned.
> Kaundinya understood,
> Three jewels are now complete.

The Buddha recited this verse once, and the eye of the teaching, free of dust, was born in Kaundinya. He was the first to become an arhat, and now the Three Jewels—Buddha, Dharma, and Sangha—were complete.

The Buddha recited the verse a second time, and the four other ascetics—Ashvajitra, Vashpa, Mahanama, and Bhadrika—gained the eye of the teaching. He recited the verse a third time and they all became arhats.

THE GROWTH OF THE SANGHA

By now eighty thousand gods had beheld the truth. Gezang donated the first temple. Yashas and five of his friends, fifty sons of city leaders, and Katyayana together with a group of five hundred men all took ordination.

Then the Buddha journeyed to Magadha. Now, the monastic community stood at sixty members. When he traveled to Uruvilva, Kashyapa, his two brothers, and an entourage of one thousand took ordination.

Shariputra and Maudgalyayana along with five hundred other men all took full monastic ordination and became arhats. The Buddha sent these two, his finest disciples, along with half of the five hundred monks to wander the countryside. The other half stayed with Kashyapa, and grew to two thousand five hundred monks. This is known as the First Council.

Anathapindada offered the Jeta Grove to the Buddha.

Then, six years after becoming enlightened, the Buddha traveled to Kapilavastu and met his father and his son. For thirteen years he stayed with them without fail in order to teach the Dharma to them.

The Nidanas, "the Episodes," along with their associated precepts, originated on the basis of Sudatta the Monk.

TEACHING THE PERFECTION OF WISDOM

Sixteen years after becoming enlightened, the Buddha was staying on Vulture Peak Mountain in Rajagriha, and he taught the four classes of monastics—full monks, novice monks, full nuns, and novice nuns. In particular, there were many bodhisattvas gathered there. He employed three kinds of miracles, those of body, speech, and mind, to instruct them in the virtuous Perfection of Wisdom teachings. He gave three such teachings—large, medium, and small.

TEACHING THE KALACAKRA TANTRA

Now, when the Teacher was seventy-nine years old, on the fifteenth day of the middle month of spring, he was staying at the great and glorious Dhanyakataka Stupa. There was a mandala of Dharmadhatuvagishvara. Above that the Primordial Buddha emerged above a Kalacakra mandala of stars and planets. On that day as well the Buddha gave esoteric ritual permissions to King Suchandra, bodhisattvas, gods, and others and taught the esoteric teachings in both extensive and condensed versions.

This was certainly the case. And yet the Buddha had

great compassion within skillful means. To disciples in the learner's tradition he gave learner's teachings. To disciples in the bodhisattva tradition he taught the path of the bodhisattva, and to disciples of the tantric tradition of esoteric spells he gave only teaching in esoteric spells. One can only imagine that he must have taught without ceasing from his enlightenment to his final nirvana!

The *Praise in One Hundred and Fifty Verses* says,

> This tormented world,
> You accept as your own.

And the Teacher beheld the sufferings of the world:

> Human beings are wrapped in a veil of ignorance,
> Tied up in knots with belief in a self,
> Crushed by a mountain of arrogance,
> Scorched by flames of desire,
> Slashed by weapons of hatred,
> Unable to cross the river of birth, aging, sickness, death.

The Buddha set out to liberate people from suffering. His tongue was like magic, resting between lips like conch shells. And he sang a glorious song in a voice like that of the god Brahma.

He began to turn the wheel of Dharma and he did not stop.

THE EIGHT FAMOUS STUPAS

Now, there are eight famous shrines in praise of the Buddha.

In the city of Kapilavastu the Birth Shrine emerged when he was born.

In Rajagriha the Enlightenment Shrine emerged when he became enlightened.

In Varanasi the Wheel-Turning, or Wisdom, Shrine appeared when he turned the wheel of Dharma.

In Jeta's Grove in Shravasti the Buddha performed the Great Miracle and defeated the heretical teachers. The Heretic Defeating Shrine emerged out of a magical shrine.

There is a stupa called Descent from Heaven, created by the Thirty-Three Gods when the Teacher returned from the gods.

In Rajagriha, Devadatta stirred up dissent within the monastic community. Shariputra and Maudgalyayana brought the community together. A stupa there is called the Reconciliation Stupa. It is also called the Light Stupa or the Real Compassion Stupa.

In Vaishali the Buddha blessed the community by deciding to remain in his body for another three months. The Victory Stupa, or Blessing Stupa, is there.

In Kushinagara the Dharma Victory Without Suffering Stupa, otherwise known as the Nirvana Stupa, appeared when the Buddha entered parinirvana.

There are also eight great reliquary shrines into which are placed the eight portions of the Buddha's remains.

There are many other stupas as well. There is a set of eleven stupas, which includes the one made out of burnt cotton, one made of unburnt cotton, and one made of charcoal. There is a stupa of the Buddha's eyetooth that was carried away by the gods and demons. There are also stupas for the Buddha's hair and fingernails, stupas for his robes, and one to wish for his return. However, the principal shrines are the eight listed above, for they include all the other types.

HOLY DAYS FOR THE BUDDHA

The correct holiday calendar for the Buddha's life is as follows:

The holiday commemorating when he entered his mother's womb, when he was born, when he achieved enlightenment, and when he died is on the fifteenth day of the fourth month.

The great holiday commemorating when he turned the wheel of Dharma of the four noble truths is on the fourth day of the sixth month.

The great holiday commemorating when he descended from heaven is on the fifteenth day of the ninth month.

The great holiday commemorating when he performed miracles at Shravasti is from the first day to the fifteenth day of the first month.

There are three auspicious days each month: The holiday commemorating when the Medicine Buddha and Prince Thotsé came into the world is on the eighth day.

The holiday commemorating when the Buddha Amitayus and Indra, lord of the gods, came into the world is on the fifteenth day.

The holiday commemorating when the Buddha Shakyamuni and the many-headed Brahma, lord of the five classes of living beings, came into the world and beheld it is on the new moon, the thirtieth day.

The factor for increasing virtue on the holy days is, in the ultimate sense, beyond number. For pedagogical purposes, however, on holy days one act is transformed into one hundred million. In a solar eclipse one act becomes billions. Within a month there are seventy million. On the three good days each act is increased by a factor of one hundred.

The holy days are times that the Buddha teaches modesty, and those wishing to attain enlightenment should be diligent in virtuous work.

THE BUDDHA'S CAREER IN BRIEF

Now, in order to appear to us, the Lord Buddha lived in Kapilavastu for twenty-nine years.

He practiced austerities for six years.

He lived in Rajagriha for five years.

He lived in Shravasti for twenty-three years.

He lived in the medicinal forests for four years.

He lived in the Cave of Fire for two years.

He lived for one year in each of the following places: Kashika, Vaishali, Pandubhumi, Kapilavastu, Venuvana, the wilderness, Balaghna, Ucirayici, the realm of the gods, Kaushambi, and Yuldra.

In total, the Buddha lived for eighty years.

The Ornament for the Thousand-Light Eon, the Life Story of Lord Victor Shakyamuni.

Act Eleven.

Turning the wheel of Dharma.

CHAPTER TWELVE

DEATH

Reverse the system with the four meditations,
Presenting the drama of final nirvana,
You danced to the music of pervasive enlightenment.
Accomplished friend of the sun, to you I bow.

Now, the Lord Buddha was endowed with great compassion. He trained living beings who were disciples in this world of five troubles. In reality the Buddha existed as the embodiment of omniscient wisdom. Yet ordinary people, who have not ascended to this state, do not have the good fortune to actually encounter that body, for they have not accumulated enough merit. The Buddha therefore considered putting his final nirvana to this great purpose. He decided to sleep in the expanse of the great city of nirvana, and he proceeded to make it so.

The *Praise in One Hundred and Fifty Verses* says,

> Out of compassion for the world,
> You taught the Dharma for a long time.
> You mentored many good students,
> Able to assist the three worlds.
>
> You trained hosts of disciples,
> Leading up to Subhadra.

And now what more remains to you
Of your debt to sentient beings?

With diamond concentration you
Grind your remains into the dust.
And even at the very end,
You do not cease austerities.

And to this unbelieving world,
You taught passage from suffering.

ANANDA'S FAILURE

Lord Shakyamuni settled in the Amra Grove in Vaishali, where he continued to work for the benefit of living beings.

"Ananda, if it is appropriate," the Buddha said, "one who has practiced a great deal of meditation in reliance upon the four magical powers may, if he wishes, live for an eon. He may even live for more than an eon!

"The Transcendent One," he said again to Ananda, "who has practiced meditation in reliance upon the four magical powers may, if the Transcendent One wishes, live for an eon. He may even live for more than an eon!"

A second time and a third time the Buddha encouraged Ananda. Ananda, however, was bound by the demon Mara and would not utter a word.

THE LAST TEACHING TO MARA

Then wicked Mara appeared.

"The Lord has lived on the earth for a long time," he said. "You have converted as many people as there are grains of sand in the River Ganga. It would be fitting for you to completely pass from the cycle of rebirth now. This body of yours is old. You should enter nirvana."

The Lord picked up a bit of earth and held it between his nails.

"Evil, sinful demon, which is greater, the soil upon the great earth or the soil upon my fingernail?" he said.

"There is a great deal of soil upon the great earth, while there is not much soil upon your fingernail," replied the sinful demon.

"The living beings whom I have trained are like the soil on my nail," said the Buddha. "Those who I have not trained are like the great earth. Three months from now I will pass completely from suffering."

Wicked Mara was overjoyed by the Buddha's words, and he went away.

The Lord began to transform the elements that constitute life. He began to give up this life. And as he was doing this, the ground rumbled. Comets fell. Every quarter of the earth blazed.

Now, Ananda and all of the disciples heard the news that the Transcendent One was going to enter final nirvana. From their hearts they lamented. They were stricken by misery and much tormented.

At length, the Buddha went to Kushinagara. Cunda the blacksmith's son prepared a final meal for him, and he ate. He then converted his last disciples, including Sunanda, whom he converted as a gandarva.

It was at this time that noble Shariputra thought, "I will not see the Transcendent One pass into nirvana." Then he rose high into the air. Flames emitted from his body. And as he burned, he passed from suffering. And eighty thousand defenders, as well as Maudgalyayana and another seventy thousand defenders, passed from suffering.

THE TEACHING TO ANANDA

"Ananda, in the final part of this night I will pass completely from suffering," said the Lord to Ananda. "You must build a cot between two Sala trees for the Transcendent One. He will sleep upon it on his right side, like a lion."

The Buddha spoke of this and other things, and Ananda wept and wept. His tears flowed down, and he wailed in lament.

"Ananda, do not suffer," said the Lord. "Do not utter laments. Whatever exists, arises, is constructed or conceived will as a matter of course fall apart. Where is there a thing that will not fall apart? Such a thing does not exist."

For a moment Ananda stood in reverence before the Transcendent One. And the Buddha spoke of great import again and soothed Ananda's thoughts. Ananda finished weeping and ceased his lament. And as he built the cot for the Transcendent One he spoke these verses.

> "The cot of the lion, great subduer,
> Is the last to be made, today.
> The cot of the lion, best of men,
> There will be no more set out.
>
> The best of men is passing from pain,
> Protector of the world is passing.
> When I look at this empty grove of Sala trees,
> I see that this is so.
>
> I'll not see our leader again.
> In this grove of Sala trees,
> This god who lived on perpetually—
> How will he ever come again?

> Alas, compounded things are impermanent,
> They are like illusions in a dream,
> A teacher such as this, a hero,
> Will pass away just like this."

Then the Lord went over to the cot that Ananda had prepared and lay down like a lion on his right side. And as he did so every plant in the entire world, from the forest trees down to the smallest seedling, inclined and bowed toward the Transcendent One, who was passing from suffering. These and other wondrous visions were beyond measure, exceeding description. Then the Buddha entrusted the teachings to sixteen great elders for as long as it takes the Protector Maitreya to arrive at Vajrasana, appointing them as his representatives.

Ananda asked why the Buddha was going to die here, in this country.

"Six previous wheel-turning kings, such as Sudharshana, passed away here," said the Buddha. "And now the Buddha makes seven."

RAHULA'S JOURNEY

Now, the Buddha's son, Rahula, could not bear to see the Lord passing from suffering, so he vanished from the Sala grove. And from the Sala grove he traveled to one of the ten world realms, the world realm known as Marici, Ray of Light. There he went before the Transcendent One named Durasada. He clasped his hands in homage, though he was distraught.

"Rahula, you must not be miserable," said the perfect Buddha when they were together. "Do not lament. Why?

You *will* become separated from that which is dear, all that is pleasing. You *will* lose it.

"Rahula, Lord Shakyamuni is at this moment lying on his right side between a pair of Sala trees. Tonight, in the final watch, he will pass from suffering. You must go there. You truly need to go there, Rahula. Go or you will certainly regret it after the Buddha completely passes from suffering!"

"I cannot even bear to hear the words 'Tonight, in the final watch, he will pass from suffering,'" said Rahula. "How can I possibly consider actually seeing him pass from suffering? There is no possibility that I can go back there!"

And Rahula vanished from that Buddha realm. He traveled through the world realms above Ray of Light and finally arrived at the tenth world. There he came before a perfect Buddha named Sarthavaha. Tears streamed from his cheeks as he lamented.

"Rahula, you must not be miserable," said the perfect Buddha when they were together. "Do not lament."

> The nature of birth is no birth.
> The nature of aging is no aging.
> The nature of illness is no illness.
> The nature of death is no death.
> The nature of diminishing is no diminishing.

> Where does a state such as this exist? It is rare.

"Rahula, every Buddha and learner became free and passed from suffering long ago," said the Buddha Sarthavaha.

"So do not suffer, Rahula. Do not lament. Look one last time upon the great king of the Shakyas. Go to clasp your hands in homage. Go to pay your respects. Go or you will certainly regret it!

"Rahula, the Transcendent One is at this moment lying on his right side like a lion in the Sala tree grove. He wishes to see you! It is clear you must go to him, Rahula."

"If I cannot bear to even hear the words 'Shakyamuni is completely passing from suffering,'" Rahula said, "how could I possibly bear witnessing it? When I hear that 'the Lord Shakyamuni, king of the Shakyas, is completely passing from suffering,' my whole body is overcome.

"How can it be that tomorrow I will be without such a great compassionate Lord? Separated from him! Without his companionship!"

"Rahula, has not the Lord said from the beginning that 'All composite things are impermanent. All compositional forces are unsatisfactory. All phenomena are without essence. Passing from suffering is peace'?" asked the perfect Buddha Sarthavaha. "The Lord Shakyamuni has answered these questions in teaching the Dharma."

"I do remember my father, Shakyamuni," said Rahula. "It is the power of his religion that causes these tears to fall.

"Tomorrow I will pray earnestly before the Lord and the monastic community, and I will witness him giving a religious teaching."

Rahula wept down to the depths of his heart. Then he was silent.

"Rahula, go before the Lord," said the perfect Buddha in encouragement. "The Lord wishes to see you. Therefore, Rahula, do not resist what I say. You will not fatigue the body of the Lord. Truly, you must be there."

Rahula folded his hands in reverence at the feet of the perfect Buddha Sarthavaha.

THE TEACHING TO RAHULA

Rahula traveled in an instant to the spot where the Lord was staying, between the pair of Sala trees. Lamenting, weeping, tears falling, he set his hands in prayer.

"Rahula, come here," said the Lord when they were together. "Rahula, do not be unhappy. Do not weep. Do not lament. Do not be depressed.

"Rahula, you have performed the duties for your father that are indeed fit for a father. And I have performed the duties for you that are fit for a son.

"Now, I am staying here to pass from suffering. I will not become your father ever again. Rahula, you will pass from suffering as well. You will not become my son ever again.

"Rahula, you and I should have no resentment toward other people. See to it, Rahula, that you and I live with no harm to any living being, with no discord."

"I beg the Lord!" Rahula pleaded with the Buddha. "Please do not completely pass from suffering!" Three times he so pleaded with the Buddha.

And the Buddha taught him—among other teachings— that passing from suffering is the reality of enlightened beings.

TEACHING TO THE ASSEMBLY

Now, the Lord spoke as well to the entire assembly of monks.

"Monks, tonight at midnight the Transcendent One will completely pass from suffering.

"Gather round, monks. This day will be the last time that I see you, the last time that I teach you.

"This day will be the last time that we look upon each other, the last time that we will come together.

"Monks, you will no longer see me. I will no longer see you. So, monks, do not be miserable, do not utter lament.

"Monks, we become separated from everything that is dear, everything that is beautiful. We become divided from them. We lose them. All compounded things are impermanent. They are suffering.

"This religion of enlightenment, which speaks of bliss, which speaks of liberation from the pain of impermanence and suffering of compounded things, is only gained through vigilance. Please, you must make efforts to be vigilant!

"Monks, this is my teaching to you."

ENTRUSTING THE TEACHING TO ANANDA

Now, the Buddha said, "Ananda, am I dear to you?"

"The Lord is dear to me," said Ananda. "The Transcendent One is dear to me."

"Ananda, if I am dear to you, give me your right hand," said the Buddha.

Ananda offered his right hand, and the Lord held it with his right hand.

"Ananda, if I am dear to you, please work for one who is dear," said the Buddha. "Ananda, over countless millions of eons I have achieved peerless, perfect, and true enlightenment. This treasury of rare and unsurpassed teachings I give to you. I entrust the teachings to you. Without doubt, you must work as I have done!

"Ananda, I entrust this treasury of supremely precious Dharma to you, so that it shall never come to harm. This is my teaching."

THE GOLDEN BODY

"Rahula, my son.
Ananda, of course!
In these two great sages,
Truly do I trust.

Now is my final night,
Upon this island earth.
Never will gods, nagas,
Humans, see me again."

The Buddha spoke these verses and other things. And after answering many questions by his miserable disciples, he said this:

"On your behalf, the Transcendent One has undertaken severe austerities for eons. He made a prayer aspiring to great compassion. And through power of that prayer he actually became awakened. He achieved peerless, perfect, and true enlightenment in this world, with its five degenerations.

"And the Transcendent One has attained an enlightened body that is indestructible, like a diamond. It has the thirty-two major and eighty minor features of enlightenment. It illuminates all of existence with endless rays of light. Simply being touched by the light, simply by viewing the body, there is no one who will not be liberated.

"The appearance of a Buddha in the world is like the udumvara flower, so rare to see. This is your last chance to behold me. Do not let it be without meaning.

"I came to this world of five kinds of trouble through the power of my ancient vow. Now that I have completed the work of training you, I draw near to passing from suffering. With single intent, you and others should look upon this body of mine, with its color of pure gold.

Furthermore, if you make earnest effort on the completely pure path, you will attain results."

The Buddha repeated this teaching three times. Then he displayed his pure, golden body to all those assembled. Then the Buddha rose again from his seat, and levitated in midair up to a height of seven Tala trees.

"I am now close to final nirvana," he said. "Gaze upon my body, the color of pure gold!"

He displayed himself in this manner a full twenty-seven times.

"I am close to completely passing from suffering," he said again to the assembly. "Look up at my body, indestructible like a diamond, unchanging like the color of pure gold. Like the udumvara flower, it is difficult to even glimpse. Know this, all of you."

Such things did the Lord say as his body became the color of pure gold.

"Behold!" Again and again he exhorted the massive assembly. Then he put his robes back upon his body.

"Now the time has come," he finally said to the assembly. "My body will delight in celestial realms."

DEATH

Employing the four concentrations in both forward and reverse orders and other inconceivable meditations, the Buddha composed himself. And as he did so, he also taught the Dharma three times to those assembled. Upon a bed decorated with precious substances he lay on his right side and went to sleep.

His head pointed north. His feet pointed south. His face looked west, and his back faced east.

He slept.

Seven precious substances and garlands of every sort also decorated the bed. At each of its four corners stood a pair of Sala trees. And the Lord rested in the four concentrations. He said nothing.

At midnight he passed completely from suffering.

Immediately the earth rumbled, meteors fell, the ten directions blazed, and the music of the gods sounded forth.

As this was happening the great Kashyapa was staying in Rajagriha. He knew that the Buddha had passed.

"This is the reality of conditioned phenomena," thought Kashyapa.

FUNERAL

"How shall we worship your remains?" Ananda had asked the Buddha earlier.

"Undertake this as you would for a wheel-turning king," instructed the Buddha.

"Wrap the body, covering it with five hundred pairs of cotton wool and new cotton. Place it in an iron tank. Fill the tank with oil, place a second tank upon it as a cover, and fire it up with a bundle of aromatic wood. Douse the fire with milk. Place the bones in a golden urn, and build a stupa at a crossroads. Worship it and create a holiday for it."

On the day after the Buddha's death, Ananda announced it to the champions of Kushinagara. The champions performed a ceremony for seven days. Then they properly laid the Buddha's bodily remains to rest.

WHEN AND WHERE IS THE BUDDHA?

The *Scripture of the Great Passage from Suffering* states that the Buddha passed away on the morning of the fifteenth day of the third month, the Vaisakha month. However, Master Shilapalita and the great scholar Shakyashri state that he passed away at midnight on the eighth day of the waxing half of the tenth month.

In reality there is no passage from suffering for the Buddha.

The *Ornament for Scriptures* states,

> A fire burns somewhere,
> And goes out elsewhere.
> People should know the Buddha,
> To come and go just so.

The Buddha has passed from suffering in this realm, yet he remains in another realm without passing. Here he has passed, for he has no disciples to whom he appears in the body of the Buddha. And yet elsewhere he has not passed, for he has disciples such as the god Indra.

"Right now he is dwelling to the east in the Buddha realm known as the Jeweled Land, as Buddha Vairocana, 'the King Bedecked with Jewels of Light.' In seven hundred uncountable eons that subduer will be our teacher," explains the *Scripture on the Contemplation of Heroic Progress*. "There are billions of worlds. In some he is being born. In some worlds he is turning the wheel of Dharma. And in other worlds he is passing from suffering."

Now, about the number of years that he lived in this realm, the *Minor Monastic Precepts* says, "Ananda, the Transcendent One has reached eighty years of age. He is old. He is exhausted."

As the *Explanation in Detail* says,

> So was he victorious, and at eighty years,
> The Supreme and Holy Sage passed away.

Nagarjuna speaks of an alternate version in his *Precious Garland*:

> Through the force of compassion,
> He comes, is born, he plays.
> He marries, renounces, practices.
> He conquers demons for enlightenment.
>
> He turns the wheel of Dharma.
> He returns from heaven.
> And so he passes from suffering.
> These are the Acts of the Buddha.

Here the act of returning from heaven is counted as a distinct act. And in the Indian city of Sankasa, the Lord traveled to the Thirty-Three Gods' Heaven to teach his mother. On the way back down he descended upon a beryl staircase. His return is known as the Descent from the Gods.

Finally scriptures such as the *Scripture on the Buddha's Skill* say that even the decline of the Dharma is also one of the Buddha's acts, even while some people claim to predict when the Buddhist religion will decline. The Buddha performed the decline so that people would not forsake the Dharma. Yet in reality the Dharma is unchanging.

CONCLUDING VERSES

> Alas! If even the word "Buddha" is rare
> In this world, to see our Precious Teacher
> Pass away from suffering in this way
> Is like casting the mind upon the wind in the sky.

Harder to glimpse than the udumvara in bloom,
The best of conquerors, the sun's friend,
The changes of your body lying upon the cot,
Who would dare imagine their ways?

An ocean of followers gathered,
Fainting, fainting, reeling on the ground,
Struck by pain, their breath begins to fade.
"Subduer! Please bless us!" they say.

Your bodily remains a Dharma wheel,
And Mahakashyapa bowed before you,
You showed your face and raised a golden hand,
You touched his head, then slept again in peace.

Before you pass from suffering magically,
The flames prepare to proffer the remains.
"Alas, that such a moment would arrive!"
Say Kaskyapa, Ananda, Brahma.

The champions did not want to burn the fire.
It lit itself through wisdom and made the remains pure,
Countless relics manifested to plant
Seeds of awakening in all living beings.

In this fearsome world of five corruptions
You alone subdued one hundred armies.
Now all Buddhas cast wondrous flowers of praise,
Drawn to your virtues, stricken with faithful thoughts.

Lord Vanquisher, I always recall the vision of your body.
Yet I am unfortunate, I think, with no chance to meet you.
My mind, a kunala bird, drops feebly
Upon the dirt, the object of its sorrow.

Best of Subduers, even hearing word
That you have passed from suffering I cannot bear.
The actual sight appearing before my eyes,
My mind cannot bear, it reels so.

The light of the past good age has sunk,
Now the darkness of a cruel age grows,
My mind is anxious, drawn down by sorrow.
Will the Lord Vanquisher no longer take me by the hand?

Supreme Teacher, a sandalwood tree suddenly fallen.
Your sons, a steadily dying tree, and in its place
Harmful people, a pile of burning sticks.
Now our hope is nowhere else. Please look upon us!

Born in this Dark Age through my past wicked deeds,
I think, Is my fortune small? And yet,
By hearing your great name the age is good,
Lord, consent to lead us to enlightenment.

Good fortune—the ship of Dharma, good passage
    to enlightenment,
Bad luck—close to the edge of the leviathan's mouth,
Uncertain—captain who comes on quick,
Will you look to us, Loving Protector?

Hearing this, Precious Teacher,
See inside our mind a bit of light from lightning,
Holding the word that you and I will be friends in
    rebirth,
Do you rejoice, good son?

In truth the Buddha passes not from suffering,
The Dharma will not fall, you teach this to those who
    hold to permanence.

In the presence of one who challenges the Subduer,
The Teacher always stands.

When you are inspired in feelings of faith,
Learned saffron-robed scholar,
Through telling the life of our leader, King of Sages,
May people be inspired in spiritual life, without sectarian
    divisions.

*The Ornament for the Thousand-Light Eon, the Life
Story of Lord Victor Shakyamuni.*

Act Twelve.

Passage from suffering.

EPILOGUE

I composed this as an aid for perpetuating the memory of this Lord Vanquisher, the Lord of Dharma, in a robust way. I abridged the words of the Buddha himself in the *Living Out of the Game Scripture,* without fabricating anything. For the episode in which the Transcendent One enters nirvana I have relied upon the *White Lotus of Compassion Scripture* and the *Great Final Nirvana Scripture.*

Two thousand seven hundred and ninety-seven years have passed since the Precious Teacher slumbered in the vast expanse of reality. And in this year (1740) I am almost forty years old.

I, the Buddhist monk Tenzin Chögyel, composed this in the Perfection of Wisdom Chapel, at the Wangdu Palace of Dharma in the capital [of Bhutan], on the Holy Day of the Descent from the Gods. I wrote with the hand of faith, ever mindful of my master, the Lord Vanquisher.

> If one ordains within the Buddhist faith,
> And does not know the life of one's Teacher,
> This is a vile, impoverished religion.
> Think upon him and develop faith.

> By virtue of this work may I never
> Be separated from the three great jewels.

With this prayer may I work for living beings,
And gain the strength of heart to help others.

In past, present, and future may I fold
My hands again and again at the feet of
Lord Vanquisher, whose unequaled kindness
Has served as a spiritual friend for me.

THE STORY OF RAHULA, THE BUDDHA'S SON

Rahula's homeland land was Kapilavastu. His family was the Shakya, whose great ancestor is Simhahanu. He was born to the daughter of Shakya Dandapani, Princess Gopa, who is also known as Yashodhara, while Shakyamuni ruled the kingdom as a bodhisattva. When the time had come for the Bodhisattva to quit the kingdom and become a renunciant, he had intercourse with Yashodhara so that no one would slander her by saying, "She is barren!" So she became pregnant.

While the Bodhisattva performed extreme ascetic practices, Yashodhara also did so, and her womb shrank. The Bodhisattva realized that such asceticism was meaningless, and he took food that was offered to him. The princess did the same things, and her womb grew.

"The princess has been raped!" the Shakya said.

"Have faith," the princess said, "I have not been raped."

And at the moment the Teacher attained enlightenment, a son was born to Yashodhara. At this moment the god Rahu held the moon in eclipse, so the boy was given the name Rahula.

Now, in order to secure Rahula to the tall stone pillar of the Bodhisattva, Yashodhara cast Rahula into a pond.

"If this boy was born from the Bodhisattva," she said, "let him fly upward!

"Let him fly all around."

And he flew right by them, as everyone there beheld this wonder.

Six years after the Buddha had become enlightened he went to meet Rahula in Kapilavastu. On the capital grounds of the city the king and the queen offered alms to him each day.

Yashodhara put a sweet into Rahula's hand.

"Hand it to your father," she said.

Now, the Teacher knew that Yashodhara would rebuff him with unpleasant words, so he emanated as five hundred Buddhas. Rahula looked upon this in wonder and made an offering to his father as the Buddha. The Buddha took the sweet and handed it back to Rahula. Rahula ate the sweet.

As the Buddha departed, Rahula followed after him. When the Buddha did not turn back, Rahula began to cry.

"This is my final life, so I cannot bear to stay," said the Buddha. "Rather, I will wander."

Rahula understood the Buddha's words, and everyone was amazed. Yashodhara's censure dissolved.

When Rahula reached the age of six, he entered the service of the Buddha. He was unwavering in his service, so King Sudhodana held a great festival for Rahula. The Buddha said to Shariputra, "Give him the ordination ritual and the novice monk's vows."

After some time he took full vows and attained the status of an arhat.

The Buddha himself went to the Heaven of the Thirty-Three Gods, and brought many celestial sons and daughters to liberation. Each gave him a crest made from their crowns, and the Noble One took these in his hands and blessed them.

"Yashodhara carried a child in her womb for six years," says a monk in a certain scripture. "Rahula remained in her womb for six years. What is the reason for this?"

"Once, Yashodhara was born as the daughter of a herdswoman," the Buddha replied. "One day this mother and daughter were taking turns carrying a full pot of buttermilk. The daughter began to falter, so she had her mother take her turn carrying the pot. As a result, this daughter would have to carry a child in the womb for six years.

"Now, Rahula was once born as King Brahmadatta. At this time there were two brothers, the sage Shanka, who was a teacher, and the sage Likhita. One day Likhita was thirsty, so he drank all of Shanka's water. He felt guilty about this and said to his elder brother the teacher, 'You must punish me!'

"'This is my brother,' said Shanka, 'and I am his teacher, so I cannot punish him.'

"'Punish me!' said Likhita again.

"'Well,' said Shanka, 'go see the king.'

"The king also said that there should be no punishment for taking the water. But Likhita persisted in asking.

"The king became angry. 'Well, wait here!'

"The king left and did not return for six days. When he returned, he said to Likhita, 'Now, get out of here!'

"And that is the reason that Rahula needed to remain in the womb for six years."

That is how the Buddha explained the causes of their karma.

As the Buddha drew near to dying, he was overwhelmed with compassion toward Rahula.

"Rahula, come here. Rahula, you must not be unhappy. Do not cry, do not despair. Rahula, you have conducted the duties due a father for your father, and I have conducted the duties due a son to my son. Now I will pass from suffering, so I will not come back as your father ever again. Rahula, you also will pass from suffering, and will never come back as my son ever again."

> It is certain, Rahula,
> My son and Ananda
> Will truly bequeath the teachings
> To the great sages.

The teachings thus passed from Rahula's hand to one hundred thousand monks, such as noble Aniruddha. Later the Buddha said to Rahula and the other Sixteen Elders, "Protect the teachings without passing into nirvana. Give the teachings."

For this reason Rahula is counted as the first of the Elders.

Furthermore, this Elder ordained such brought many forefathers such as Saraha and Kukuripa, and it is because of this that they were able to reach spiritual maturation in the tradition of secret mantra. He also disguised himself as King Visukalpa and spread the teachings of the Diamond Way, so he is the origin of this tradition as well.

This is how Rahula, the only son of the perfect Buddha—an ancestral as well as a Dharma son—became his regent, one of the Sixteen Elders. Even now he lives on the island of Priyanku, served by one thousand arhats, ever working for the benefit of living beings.

NAGARJUNA'S "PRAISE TO THE TWELVE ACTS"

I bow to Buddha Shakyamuni.
At first you think to seek enlightenment
And so you gather wisdom, gain merit.
Now, great and vast is your work for living beings.
To you, our Protector, I give praise.

You train the gods and knew now to train humans,
Down from heaven, come as an elephant,
You see a family, you see Mayadevi,
And enter her womb. To you I bow.

Ten months passed, Shakya son, and you
Are born amid the gardens of Lumbini.
Brahma, Indra, bow to your great marks,
Certain to be enlightened. To you I bow.

A virile youth, a lion among men,
At Anga Maghada you show your skill.
When laying waste to men so full of pride,
You are without match. To you I bow.

You act in accordance with the world,
Avoiding all slander, you take up wives,
You know such skillful methods will protect,
Defend the royal realms. To you I bow.

You know samsara's ways to have no heart,
And leave from home, soaring through the sky.
At the foot of a pure shrine you take
Full renunciation. To you I bow.

You toil to gain enlightenment,
Six years at the River Nairanjana.
You take to ascetic practice, and finally,
You gain great concentration. To you I bow.

To make your endless efforts meaningful,
In the Middle Country, under the Bodhi tree,
Cross-legged, still, awakened, you attain
Perfect enlightenment. To you I bow.

You quickly looked with love upon all beings,
At Varanasi, all the holy sites,
You turned the Dharma wheel for disciples,
You placed them on three paths. To you I bow.

You bested those who wrongly debate others,
Like Devadatta and the Heretics Six.
You subdued demons, frightened little servants.
A sage, victor in battle. To you I bow.

With qualities unmatched in the three worlds,
You showed great miracles at Shravasti,
All the gods and humans honored you,
Promoter of the Teaching. To you I bow.

To quickly encourage the lazy ones,
At Kusinagari you died, and yet
Your body, diamond-like, was immortal.
From suffering you passed. To you I bow.

So that his body will not come to ruin,
So future living beings may collect merit,
The Buddha manifests many relics,
Eight shares have your remains. To you I bow.

Such are the acts of the Teaching's Lord and Master,
Described and praised a bit in brief.
May what merit there is here cause all beings
To act as would the One Who's Gone to Bliss.

Glossaries

These two glossaries list the personal names and the places in *The Life of the Buddha*. There are over seventy characters in the story—gods, demons, and Buddhas, men, women, and children—as well as almost fifty place-names. Most of the persons and place-names are translated from the Tibetan into Sanskrit, for which I have relied primarily on the Sanskrit terms used in Bays's *Voice of the Buddha* and Butön's *History of Buddhism*. The Tibetan-language renderings of the terms used by Tenzin Chögyel are in parentheses.

PEOPLE

Agnidattapura (mes sbyin gyi bu). Grandson of the sage Arana. Chap. 3.

Agratejas (gzi brjid dam pa). Celestial being in Tushita Heaven. Chap. 2.

Ananda (kun dga' bo). A cousin of the young Bodhisattva. Chap. 5.

Anathapindada (mgon med zas sbyin). A layperson who offers Jeta Grove to the Buddha. Chap. 11.

Arada Kalama (sgyu rtsal shes pa'i bur ring 'phur). An early teacher of Shakyamuni. Chap. 6.

Arana (nyon mongs med). A sage who visits Shakyamuni as a child. Chap. 3.

Arati (dga' byed). One of Mara's daughters. Chap. 9.

Ashvajitra (rta thul). One of the Buddha's first five disciples. Chap. 11.

Asita (nag po). A sage living in the Himalaya Mountains who visits the Shakya kingdom to see the newly born Bodhisattva. Chap. 3.

Bhadrika (bzang ldan). One of the Buddha's first five disciples. Chap. 11.

Bimbisara (gzugs can snying po). A king of the city of Raja-griha, who offers his kingdom to the Buddha. Chap. 6.

Bodhisattva (byang chub sems dpa'). The primary epithet of the Buddha prior to his enlightenment.

Brahma (Tshangs pa). A god who requests that the Buddha teach on earth. Chap. 2 and throughout.

Buddha (sangs rgyas). The "enlightened one." The primary title of Shakyamuni after he achieved "bodhi," or enlightenment.

Buddha Dipankara (Mar me mdzad). The Buddha just prior to the current Buddha Shakyamuni. Chap. 1.

Buddha Indradvaja (dbang po rgyal mtshan). A Buddha who lived before Buddha Shakyamuni. Chap. 1.

Buddha Kashyapa ('od srungs). A past Buddha. Chap. 1.

Buddha Sadhukara (legs mdzad). A past Buddha. Chap. 1.

Buddha Vairochana (rnam par snang mdzad). A celestial Buddha identified with Buddha Shakyamuni. Chap. 1.

Chandaka ('dun pa). Shakyamuni's charioteer and friend. Chaps. 3 and 6.

Chandraprabha (zla 'od). One of Shakyamuni's previous births. Chap. 1.

Dandapani (lag na be con). Member of the Shakya clan, father of Gopa. Chap. 5.

Devadatta (lhas sbyin). Buddha Shakyamuni's cousin and rival. Chap. 5.

Gopa ('tsho ma). The wife of Shakyamuni. Chap. 5.

Indra (brgya byin). A god who becomes a disciple of the Buddha. Chap. 1 and throughout.

Kala (mi dkar ba). A sage who offers a prediction about Shakyamuni's future. Chap. 3.

Kalika (nag po). A serpent king who sees the Buddha shortly before his enlightenment. Chap. 8.

Kantaka (sgags ldan). Shakyamuni's horse. Chaps. 3 and 6.

Kashyapa ('od srungs). An early and important disciple of the Buddha. Chap. 11.

Kaundinya (kau di n.ya). One of the Buddha's first five disciples. Chap. 11.

Madhisambhava (sbrang rtsi 'byung ba). Future Buddha predicted by Buddha Shakyamuni. Chap. 10.

Mahanama (ming chen). One of the Buddha's first five disciples. Chap. 11.

Maitreya (byams pa). A bodhisattva who resides in Tushita Heaven, destined to be the next Buddha following Buddha Shakyamuni. Chaps. 1 and 12.

Maitribhadra (byams pa'i stobs). One of Shakyamuni's previous births. Chap. 1.

Mara (bdud). A demon who personifies evil, Buddha Shakyamuni's primary foe. Chap. 9 and following.

Maskari Gocaliputra (gnag lhas gyi bu kun tu rgyu). A non-Buddhist teacher. Chap. 1.

Matanga (glang po). A self-enlightened person living during the time Buddha Shakyamuni was born. Chap. 1.

Maudgalyayana (mo'u 'gal gyi bu). One of Buddha Shakyamuni's first disciples. Chaps. 11 and 12.

Mayadevi (sgyu 'phrul ma). Buddha Shakyamuni's mother. Chaps. 2 and 3.

Mucilinda (btang gzung). A serpent king who hosted Buddha Shakyamuni at his house. Chap. 10.

Nanda (dga' bo). A serpent king present at Buddha Shakyamuni's birth. Chap. 3.

Nanda (dga' bo). Shakyamuni's half brother and eventual disciple. Chap. 5.

Narada (mes byin). Asita's nephew. Chap. 3.

Prabhasa (rab gsal). A king, one of Shakyamuni's previous births. Chap. 1.

Prajapati (skye dgu'i bdag mo). Buddha Shakyamuni's stepmother. Chap. 3.

Prasannakirti (gsal grags). One of Buddha Shakyamuni's previous births. Chap. 1.

Primordial Buddha (dang po'i sangs rgyas). Buddha Shakyamuni in the form in which he taught the Kalacakra tantra. Chap. 11.

Purana Kashyapa ('od srungs rdzogs byed). A non-Buddhist teacher prior to Buddha Shakyamuni. Chap. 1.

Rahula (dgra can 'dzin). Buddha Shakyamuni's son. Chap. 12.

Raivata (rigs ldan). A brahmin whom Buddha Shakyamuni visited after he cut off his hair. Chap. 6.

Ratnagarbha (rin chen snying po). A Buddha of the distant past in front of whom Buddha Shakyamuni made his original vow to become enlightened. Chap. 1.

Sagara (rgya mtsho). A serpent king who takes Buddha Shakyamuni's bowl. Chap. 8.

Shakya (sha kya). Buddha Shakyamuni's family, traditionally held to have been a kingdom on the Himalayan foothills. Chap. 2.

Shakyamuni (sha kya thub pa). A name of the Buddha of this era, "the Sage of the Shakyas." Chaps. 5 and 12.

Shakyavardhana (sha kya 'phel). A god of the Shakya family. Chap. 3.

Shariputra (sha ri bu). One of Buddha Shakyamuni's primary disciples. Chap. 11.

Shvetaketu (dam pa tog dkar po). Name of Buddha Shakyamuni when he resided in Tushita Heaven. Chap. 1.

Siddhartha (don grub). Buddha Shakyamuni's personal name. Chap. 3.

Sudatta (bzang byin). A monk credited with compiling the Nidana literature under Buddha Shakyamuni. Chap. 11.

Suddhodana (zas gtsang). King of the Shakya tribe, Buddha Shakyamuni's father. Chap. 2.

Sujata (legs skyes ma). A village woman who provides food to Buddha Shakyamuni when he is starving. Chap. 7.

Tanha (sred ma). One of Mara's daughters. Chap. 9.

Udraka Ramaputra (rang byed kyi bu lhag spyod). An early teacher of Buddha Shakyamuni. Chap. 6.

Upananda (nyer dga'). A serpent king present at Buddha Shakyamuni's birth. Chap. 3.

Vagishvarakirti (ngag gi dbang phyug grags pa). A later Indian author of tantric works, cited in *The Life of the Buddha*. Chap. 1.

Vaishravana (rnam thos sras). One of the four guardian kings. Chaps. 3 and 10.

Vajradhatu (rdo rje dbyings). Name of Buddha Shakyamuni.

Vajragarbha (rdo rje snying po). Bodhisattva who teaches the *Scripture of the Ten Grounds* at Buddha Shakyamuni's request. Chap. 10.

Vashpa (rlangs pa). One of the Buddha's first five disciples. Chap. 11.

Vishnu (gu lang). A god who praises Buddha Shakyamuni when he is a child. Chap. 3.

Vishvamitra (kun gyi bshes gnyen). Buddha Shakyamuni's language instructor. Chap. 4.

Yashodhara (grags 'dzin ma or grags ldan mo). Another name for the wife of the Buddha along with Gopa ('tsho ma). Chap. 3.

PLACES

Akanishta Heaven ('og min). Celestial realm where the Buddha is said in some accounts to have achieved enlightenment. Chap. 7.

Anala (tsan da la). Town through which Buddha Shakyamuni travels. Chap. 11.

Arrow Well (mda'i khron pa). Place where Buddha Shakyamuni's arrow landed during an archery competition. Chap. 5.

Balaghna (byis pa gsod). Place where the Buddha spends one year after enlightenment. Chap. 11.

Dhanyakataka Stupa ('bras spungs rgyal ba'i mchod rten). Place where Buddha Shakyamuni taught the Kalacakra tantra at the age of seventy-nine. Chap. 11.

Golangagulaparivartana Hill (ma bgyur ba'i ri). Place where the self-enlightened non-Buddhist Matanga lived when Buddha Shakyamuni was born. Chap. 1.

Heaven of the Thirty-Three Gods (sum cu rtsa gsum). Celestial realm where Buddha Shakyamuni's mother resides. Chap. 3.

Heretic Defeating Shrine (mu stegs pham mdzad kyi mchod rten). Stupa that emerged miraculously in Shravasti when Buddha Shakyamuni defeated non-Buddhist challengers. Chap. 11.

Himalaya Mountains (ri go gangs can). Mountain range to the north of Kapilavastu, home of the sage Asita. Chap. 3.

Immaculate Shrine (mchod rten rnam dag). Place where Buddha Shakyamuni cut off his hair. Chap. 6.

Jambudvipa ('dzam bu'i gling). The "Rose Apple Continent," India. Chap. 1.

Jeta Grove (rgyal byed tshal). The park offered to Buddha Shakyamuni by Anathapindada. Chap. 11.

Kapilavastu (ser skya'i yul). Buddha Shakyamuni's hometown. Chap. 3 and throughout.

Kashika (ka shi ka). Place where the Buddha spends one year after enlightenment. Chap. 11.

Kushinagara (rtswa mchog grong khyer). Place where the Buddha died. Chap. 12.

Lumbini (lum bi ni). Birthplace of Buddha Shakyamuni. Chap. 2.

Magadha (ma ga dha). Major region of Buddha Shakyamuni's teaching career. Its capital was Rajagriha. Chap. 11.

Mount Gaya (ri ga ya). Place where the Buddha began to learn meditation with five ascetic companions. Chap. 7.

Mount Pandava (ri skya bo). Place the Buddha traveled through right after his renunciation. Chap. 6.

Mount Sarvadhara (ri bo kun 'dzin). Home of the sage Arana. Chap. 3.

Nirvana Stupa (myang 'das mchod rten). Stupa in Kushinagara where the Buddha died. Chap. 11.

Pandubhumi (sa dkar can). Place where the Buddha spends one year after enlightenment. Chap. 11.

Rajagriha (rgyal po'i khab). Capital of the Magadha region, ruled by the Buddha's patron King Bimbisara. Chap. 6 and throughout.

Rishipatana (drang srong lhung ba). Place where Buddha Shakyamuni taught his first sermon, also known as Deer Park. Chaps. 1 and 11.

River Ganga (gang ga). Buddha Shakyamuni crosses the river on the way to give his first sermon. Chap. 11.

River Nairanjana (nai ranydza na). A major river along which the Buddha practiced austerities. Chap. 7.

Sala Cave (sa la'i phug). Place where Buddha Shakyamuni performed miracles after his enlightenment. Chap. 10.

Sarathi (kha lo sgyur). Town through which Buddha Shakyamuni travels. Chap. 11.

Shravasti (mnyan yod). Major city in Buddha Shakyamuni's life, the home to his major patron Anathapindada, and where he spent twenty-three rainy seasons, according to some sources. Chap. 11.

Shrine of the Saffron Robe Reception (ngur smrig blangs pa'i mchod rten). Stupa commemorating Buddha Shakyamuni's first robes as a renunciant. Chap. 6.

Tushita Heaven (dga' ldan). The heavenly realm where Buddha Shakyamuni lived prior to his birth in the Shakya family. Chap. 1.

Ucirayici (mchod rten ri). Place where the Buddha spends one year after enlightenment. Chap. 11.

Uruvilva (lteng rgyas). Town through which Buddha Shakyamuni travels. Chap. 11.

Vaishali (yangs pa can). Place where the Buddha spends one year after enlightenment. Chap. 11.

Vajrasana (rdo rje gdan). The "Diamond Throne," the place where Buddha Shakyamuni achieved enlightenment. Chaps. 8 and 12.

Varanasi (wa ra ṇa si, ka shi ka, gsal ldan). Major city in the Buddha's career. Chaps. 2 and following.

Vulture Peak Mountain (bya rgod phung po'i ri). Major teaching site of Buddha Shakyamuni near the city of Rajagriha. Chap. 12.

Notes

These notes provide references to Tenzin Chögyel's Tibetan text at the beginning of each chapter, as well as references to all of the verses quoted in his *Life of the Buddha*. For readers who wish to compare Tenzin Chögyel's version of the narrative with those of his predecessors, the notes provide references to the two most important sources of *The Life of the Buddha*, the *Living Out of the Game Scripture*, translated in Gwendolyn Bays, *The Voice of the Buddha*, and Butön's *History of Buddhism*, translated by Eugene Obermiller. The Tibetan text translated here as Tenzin Chögyel's *Life of the Buddha* is: Bstan 'dzin chos rgyal (1701–1767), *Bcom ldan 'das rgyal ba sha'akya thub pa'i rnam par thar pa bskal bzang sgron ma stong gi mdzes rgyan*, in *Masterpieces of Bhutanese Biographical Literature*. New Delhi, 1970, pp. 245–349: pp. 246.1–249.1.

CHAPTER ONE: HEAVEN

3 **Heaven:** Tibetan text: pp. 249.1–262.2. Bays, *The Voice of the Buddha*, chapters 1–5.

3 *Scripture of the Era of Good: Bskal pa bzang po pa zhes bya ba theg pa chen po'i mdo*. Sde dge Bka' 'gyur, Mdo sde, vol. Ka, fol. 1b1–340a5 (Hakuji Ui et al., *A Complete Catalog of the Tibetan Buddhist Canons* [Sendai: Tōhuko

Imperial University, 1934], no. 94). Full translation in
*The Fortunate Aeon: How the Thousand Buddhas
Became Enlightened.* Berkeley, CA: Dharma Publishing,
1986: vol. 4, p. 1745. See Butön's *History of Buddhism:*
E. Obermiller, translator, *History of Buddhism (Chosh-
byung) by Bu-ston, I. Part, The Jewelry of Scripture.*
Heidelberg: Harrassowitz, 1931. *II. Part, The History of
Buddhism in India and Tibet:* vol. 1, p. 90.

4 **A wonder it is that ignorance:** Aśvaghoṣa, *Letter of Con-
solation. Mya ngan bsal ba.* Sde dge Bstan 'gyur, Spring
yig, vol. Nge, fol. 33a2–34a3 (*Complete Catalog of the
Tibetan Buddhist Canons,* no. 4177): fol. 34a.

4 **The snake is pleased resting in his hole:** Source unidenti-
fied.

5 **Who goes for refuge in Buddha:** *The Pig's Tale. Phag
mo'i rtogs pa brjod pa zhes bya ba'i mdo.* Sde dge Bka'
'gyur, Mdo sde, vol. AM, 289b2–291a7 (*Complete
Catalog of the Tibetan Buddhist Canons,* no. 345).
Translation in Andy Rotmann, translator, *Divine Stories:
Divyavadana Part I.* Somerville, MA: Wisdom Publications, 2008, p. 327.

5 **If you are a thinking being:** *Praise in One Hundred and
Fifty Verses.* D. R. Shackleton Bailey, *The Śatapañcāśatka
of Mātṛceta.* Cambridge, UK: Cambridge University
Press, 1951, verse 2. Rta dbyangs, *Brgya lnga bcu pa zhes
bya ba'i bstod pa.* Sde dge Bstan 'gyur, Bstod tshogs, vol.
Ka, 110a3–116a5: fol. 110a (*Complete Catalog of the
Tibetan Buddhist Canons,* no. 1147).

5 *Praise Exceeding the Gods:* Shamkarapati. *Lha las phul
du byung bar bstod pa* by Bde byed bdag po. Sde dge
Bstan 'gyur, Bstod tshogs, vol. Ka, fol. 43b4–45a3: 44b
(*Complete Catalog of the Tibetan Buddhist Canons,* no.
1112). Translation in *The Sublime Path of the Victorious
Ones: A Book of Mahayana Prayers.* Dharamsala: Library
of Tibetan Works and Archives, 1981.

7 **the brahmin Samudrarenu:** *Snying rje pad ma dkar po
zhes bya ba theg pa chen po'i mdo* (*Complete Catalog of
the Tibetan Buddhist Canons,* no. 112). The story of
Samudrarenu occurs in chapter 3. A summary may be
found in Isshi Yamada, *Karuṇāpuṇḍarīka.* London: School
of Oriental and African Studies, 1968.

7   **When I was in a lowly earlier life:** *Bskal pa bzang po pa zhes bya ba theg pa chen po'i mdo.* Sde dge Bka' 'gyur, Mdo sde, vol. Ka, fol. 1b1–340a5: fol. 288a.4 (*Complete Catalog of the Tibetan Buddhist Canons,* no. 94). Butön, *History of Buddhism,* vol. 1, p. 108.

7   *Scripture of Returning Kindness: Thabs mkhas pa chen po sangs rgyas drin lan bsab pa'i mdo.* Sde dge Bka' 'gyur, Mdo sde, vol. A, 86a2–198b7 (*Complete Catalog of the Tibetan Buddhist Canons,* no. 353). Butön, *History of Buddhism,* vol. 1, p. 108.

7   *Scripture of the White Lotus of Compassion:* Isshi Yamada, *Karuṇāpuṇḍarīka,* London: School of Oriental and African Studies, 1968. Butön, *History of Buddhism,* vol. 1, p. 108.

7   *Scripture of the Three Collections: Phung po gsum pa zhes bya ba theg pa chen po'i mdo.* Sde dge Bka' 'gyur, Mdo sde, vol. Ya, 57a3–77a3 (*Complete Catalog of the Tibetan Buddhist Canons,* no, 284). Partial translation in Brian Beresford, translator, *Mahayana Purification.* Dharamsala: Library of Tibetan Works and Archives, 1980, pp. 17–21. Butön, *History of Buddhism,* vol. 1, p. 108.

8   **To lead afflicted people out:** Shackleton Bailey, *The Śatapañcāśatka of Mātṛceta,* verse 129.

9   **Through three immeasurable eons you:** Shackleton Bailey, *The Śatapañcāśatka of Mātṛceta,* verse 26.

9   **Bedecked with jewels of every kind:** It is clear that Tenzin Chögyel borrowed this verse from Butön's *History of Buddhism,* vol. 1, p. 131. Butön also takes the verse to be from *The Descent into Lanka Scripture,* yet although the verse appears in many canonical and Tibetan works, it is not found in the canonical version of *The Descent into Lanka.*

9   **He knew the highest truth in Akanishta:** Ngag gi dbang phyug grags pa, *'Chi ba slu ba'i man ngag.* Sde dge Bstan 'gyur, Rgyud, vol. Sha (*Complete Catalog of the Tibetan Buddhist Canons,* no. 1748). Butön, *History of Buddhism,* vol. 1, p. 136.

10 **"With virtues vast, you're mindful, understanding":** *Rgya cher rol pa zhes bya ba theg pa chen po'i mdo.* Sde sde Bka' 'gyur, Mdo sde, vol. Kha, fol. 1b1–216b7: 8a (*Complete Catalog of the Tibetan Buddhist Canons,* no. 95).

Translation in Bays, translator, *The Voice of the Buddha: The Beauty of Compassion*. Berkeley, CA: Dharma Publishing, 1983. Two volumes. Translated from the French, vol. 1, pp. 23–25.

12 **"A single lion defeats a herd of beasts":** *Mngon par byung ba'i mdo.* Sde dge Bka' 'gyur, Mdo sde, vol. Sa, fol. 1b1– 125a7: 6b (*Complete Catalog of the Tibetan Buddhist Canons*, no. 301). Butön, *History of Buddhism*, vol. 2, p. 10.

12 **When from this supreme place of Tushita:** Bays, *The Voice of the Buddha*, vol. 1, p. 65. Butön, *History of Buddhism*, vol. 2, p. 8.

CHAPTER TWO: DESCENT

15 **Descent:** Tibetan text: pp. 262.2–266.3. Bays, *The Voice of the Buddha*, chapters 5 and 6.

16 **A cap of woven gold, a red crown:** Butön, *History of Buddhism*, vol. 2, p. 10. Bays, *The Voice of the Buddha*, vol. 1, p. 96.

CHAPTER THREE: BIRTH

19 **Birth:** Tibetan text: pp. 266.3–274.4. Bays, *The Voice of the Buddha*, chapters 7 and 8.

22 **"I see the omens of this newborn babe":** Butön, *History of Buddhism*, vol. 2, p. 14. Compare Bays, *The Voice of the Buddha*, vol. 1, p. 150.

23 **"His private parts now hidden in a sheath":** Butön, *History of Buddhism*, vol. 2, p. 14.

23 **"Have all of a thousand suns":** Butön, *History of Buddhism*, vol. 2, p. 13. *Mngon par byung ba'i mdo,* fol. 15a.

23 **"The rays of sun are very sharp":** Butön, *History of Buddhism*, vol. 2, p. 13. *Mngon par byung ba'i mdo,* fol. 15a.

23 **"Great King, we have traveled here":** Butön, *History of Buddhism*, vol. 2, p. 13. *Mngon par byung ba'i mdo,* fol. 15b.

24 **"The well-bred horse":** Butön, *History of Buddhism*, vol. 2, p. 13. *Mngon par byung ba'i mdo,* fol. 15b.

24 **"Oh Lord, the pundits are mistaken":** Butön, *History of Buddhism*, vol. 2, p. 13. *Mngon par byung ba'i mdo,* fol. 16a.

24 *Scripture on Recalling the Buddha:* Not located.
25 **"The sages offer prayers to you":** *Rgya cher rol pa zhes bya ba theg pa chen po'i mdo,* fol. 58b. Bays, *The Voice of the Buddha,* vol. 1, p. 158.
25 **Who has so many qualities:** Shackleton Bailey, *The Śatapañcāśatka of Mātṛceta,* verse 8.

CHAPTER FOUR: EDUCATION

27 **Education:** Tibetan text: pp. 274.4–277.3. Bays, *The Voice of the Buddha,* chapters 9–11.
27 **"This person is quite wonderful!":** *Rgya cher rol pa zhes bya ba theg pa chen po'i mdo,* fol. 67a. Bays, *The Voice of the Buddha,* vol. 1, p. 188. Butön, *History of Buddhism,* vol. 2, p. 13.
28 **"He comes as a great sea to cool":** Bays, *The Voice of the Buddha,* vol. 1, p. 202.
28 **"At the time that you were born":** Bays, *The Voice of the Buddha,* vol. 1, p. 204. Butön, *History of Buddhism,* vol. 2, p. 15.

CHAPTER FIVE: HAREM

31 **Harem:** Tibetan text: pp. 277.3–284.3. Bays, *The Voice of the Buddha,* chapter 12.
31 **"Its faults are quite well-known to me, desire":** Bays, *The Voice of the Buddha,* vol. 1, p. 212. Butön, *History of Buddhism,* vol. 2, p. 16.
32 **"The lotus blooms within the muddy pool":** Bays, *The Voice of the Buddha,* vol. 1, p. 212. Butön, *History of Buddhism,* vol. 2, p. 16.
32 **"Brahmin, these qualities I do possess":** Bays, *The Voice of the Buddha,* vol. 1, p. 216. Butön, *History of Buddhism,* vol. 2, p. 17.
33 **"These women are great liars, trust them not!":** Bays, *The Voice of the Buddha,* vol. 1, p. 216. Butön, *History of Buddhism,* vol. 2, p. 18.

CHAPTER SIX: RENUNCIATION

37   **Renunciation:** Tibetan text: pp. 284.3–295.3. Bays, *The Voice of the Buddha,* chapters 13–16.

37   **"You once beheld the hundred human ills":** Bays, *The Voice of the Buddha,* vol. 1, p. 243. Butön, *History of Buddhism,* vol. 2, p. 21.

38   **"The pain of age and illness burns the worlds":** Bays, *The Voice of the Buddha,* vol. 1, p. 259. Butön, *History of Buddhism,* vol. 2, p. 21.

38   **"A voice so sweet, a voice so soft":** Bays, *The Voice of the Buddha,* vol. 1, p. 279. Butön, *History of Buddhism,* vol. 2, p. 22.

39   **"Charioteer, this man is weak and slight":** Bays, *The Voice of the Buddha,* vol. 1, p. 285. Butön, *History of Buddhism,* vol. 2, p. 23.

39   **"My only god, this man is beat by age":** Bays, *The Voice of the Buddha,* vol. 1, p. 286. Butön, *History of Buddhism,* vol. 2, p. 23.

40   **"I must go back, do turn this chariot quick":** Bays, *The Voice of the Buddha,* vol. 1, p. 286. Butön, *History of Buddhism,* vol. 2, p. 26.

40   **"If only age and death would disappear!":** Bays, *The Voice of the Buddha,* vol. 1, p. 289. Butön, *History of Buddhism,* vol. 2, p. 26.

40   **"This you describe I now desire as well":** Bays, *The Voice of the Buddha,* vol. 1, p. 290. Butön, *History of Buddhism,* vol. 2, p. 26.

42   **"Oh, how all of these creatures suffer so!":** Bays, *The Voice of the Buddha,* vol. 1, p. 311. Butön, *History of Buddhism,* vol. 2, p. 28.

43   **"Good fortune this is! I will attain my goals":** Bays, *The Voice of the Buddha,* vol. 1, p. 316. Butön, *History of Buddhism,* vol. 2, p. 29.

43   **"I seek the welfare of all living beings":** Bays, *The Voice of the Buddha,* vol. 1, p. 329. Butön, *History of Buddhism,* vol. 2, p. 29.

44   **"Until I've reached the supreme path":** Bays, *The Voice of the Buddha,* vol. 1, p. 335.

CHAPTER SEVEN: AUSTERITY

47 **Austerity:** Tibetan text: pp. 295.3–300.1. Bays, *The Voice of the Buddha*, chapter 17.

48 **Sitting in a meditation position upon unswept ground:** Compare Rupert Gethin, translator, *Sayings of the Buddha: A Selection of Suttas from the Pali Nikāyas*. Oxford and New York: Oxford University Press, 2008, p. 181.

49 **"Sun and moon and stars may fall to earth":** Bays, *The Voice of the Buddha*, vol. 2, p. 386. Butön, *History of Buddhism*, vol. 2, p. 33.

49 **Now, the Bodhisattva's limbs:** Compare Gethin, *Sayings of the Buddha*, p. 183.

50 **"Where perfect Buddhas dwell, Buddhas awake":** Butön, *History of Buddhism*, vol. 1, p. 131. This verse appears in many Buddhist scriptures and treatises. Butön cites it as a quote from *The Descent into Lanka Scripture*. *Lang kar gshegs pa'i theg pa chen po'i mdo*. Sde dge Bstan 'gyur, Mdo sde, vol. Ca, fol. 56a1–191b7 (*Complete Catalog of the Tibetan Buddhist Canons*, no. 107). However, the verse does not appear in the Tibetan translation of this scripture.

CHAPTER EIGHT: THE DIAMOND THRONE

53 **The Diamond Throne:** Tibetan text: pp. 300.1–304.5. Bays, *The Voice of the Buddha*, chapters 18–20.

55 **"Oh, Svastika, please, quick, give me some grass":** Bays, *The Voice of the Buddha*, vol. 2, p. 435. Butön, *History of Buddhism*, vol. 2, p. 35.

55 **My body may wither upon this seat—okay:** Bays, *The Voice of the Buddha*, vol. 2, p. 439. Butön, *History of Buddhism*, vol. 2, p. 35.

CHAPTER NINE: DEMONS

57 **Demons:** Tibetan text: pp. 304.5–309.1. Bays, *The Voice of the Buddha*, chapter 21.

57 "That noble being, who labored many eons": Bays, *The Voice of the Buddha,* vol. 2, p. 458. Butön, *History of Buddhism,* vol. 2, p. 36.

58 "Tormentors, ghouls, and serpent shapes": Bays, *The Voice of the Buddha,* vol. 2, p. 467. Butön, *History of Buddhism,* vol. 2, p. 36.

58 "The king of the Shakya knows reality": Bays, *The Voice of the Buddha,* vol. 2, p. 469. Butön, *History of Buddhism,* vol. 2, p. 36.

58 "Endless sacrifice I've made before!": Bays, *The Voice of the Buddha,* vol. 2, p. 481. Butön, *History of Buddhism,* vol. 2, p. 37, which includes a different version of this verse.

58 "This earth is witness for all living beings": Bays, *The Voice of the Buddha,* vol. 2, p. 482. Butön, *History of Buddhism,* vol. 2, p. 37.

59 They heard these words, wicked Mara and his troops: Bays, *The Voice of the Buddha,* vol. 2, p. 483. Butön, *History of Buddhism,* vol. 2, p. 38.

CHAPTER TEN: ENLIGHTENMENT

61 Enlightenment: Tibetan text: pp. 309.1–315.4. Bays, *The Voice of the Buddha,* chapters 22–24.

62 "Virtue brings bliss, it removes every pain": Bays, *The Voice of the Buddha,* vol. 2, p. 531. Butön, *History of Buddhism,* vol. 2, p. 39.

62 At the heart of the earth, where: Bays, *The Voice of the Buddha,* vol. 2, p. 561.

62 *The Vast Array of the Buddha:* The Tibetan name for the *Flower Ornament Scripture: Sangs rgyas phal po che zhes bya ba shin tu rgyas pa chen po'i mdo.* Sde dge Bstan 'gyur, Phal chen, vol. Ka, fol. 1b1–a 363a6 (*Complete Catalog of the Tibetan Buddhist Canons,* no. 44). *The Scripture of the Ten Grounds* is chapter 31 of the version of the *Flower Ornament Scripture* that was translated into Tibetan, and sometimes circulated as an independent scripture. Likewise, *The Design of Samantabhadra's Realm* is the final devotional section of chapter 45.

64 "One who hears and sees the faith finds joy": Bays, *The Voice of the Buddha*, vol. 2, p. 575. Butön, *History of Buddhism*, vol. 2, p. 40.

64 "You give a bowl to a Transcendent One": Bays, *The Voice of the Buddha*, vol. 2, p. 579. Butön, *History of Buddhism*, vol. 2, p. 40.

65 "You who work the gods' blessing": Bays, *The Voice of the Buddha*, vol. 2, p. 584. Butön, *History of Buddhism*, vol. 2, p. 40.

CHAPTER ELEVEN: TEACHING

67 Teaching: Tibetan text: pp. 315.4–327.4. Bays, *The Voice of the Buddha*, chapters 25 and 26.

67 I have attained an essential Dharma: Bays, *The Voice of the Buddha*, vol. 2, p. 594. Butön, *History of Buddhism*, vol. 2, p. 41.

67 "My love for all the world knows no bounds": Bays, *The Voice of the Buddha*, vol. 2, p. 595. Butön, *History of Buddhism*, vol. 2, p. 41.

68 "Here in Magadha low teachings reign": Bays, *The Voice of the Buddha*, vol. 2, p. 602. Butön, *History of Buddhism*, vol. 2, p. 42.

68 "Brahma, people now in Magadha": Bays, *The Voice of the Buddha*, vol. 2, p. 605. Butön, *History of Buddhism*, vol. 2, p. 43.

68 "I do not have a master": Bays, *The Voice of the Buddha*, vol. 2, pp. 615–616. Butön, *History of Buddhism*, vol. 2, p. 43.

72 Just so, with twelve aspects: Bays, *The Voice of the Buddha*, vol. 2, pp. 615–616. Butön, *History of Buddhism*, vol. 2, p. 46.

74 This tormented world: *Praise in One Hundred and Fifty Verses*. Shackleton Bailey, *The Śatapañcāśatka of Mātṛceta*, verse 10c–d.

74 Human beings are wrapped in a veil of ignorance: Butön, *History of Buddhism*, vol. 2, p. 56.

77 the Lord Buddha lived in Kapilavastu for twenty-nine years: This list of places is a reorganization of a list quoted in Butön, *History of Buddhism*, vol. 1, p. 70, which Butön attributes to the *Mahāvibhāṣā*.

CHAPTER TWELVE: DEATH

79 **Death:** Tibetan text: pp. 327.4–347.5.

79 **The *Praise in One Hundred and Fifty Verses*:** Shackleton Bailey, *The Śatapañcāśatka of Mātṛceta*, verses 142–144, 145c–d.

82 **"The cot of the lion, great subduer":** *Scripture on the Concentrations of the Four Youths, Khye'u bzhi'i ting nge 'dzin ces bya ba theg pa chen po'i mdo.* Sde dge Bka' 'gyur, Mdo sde, vol. Na 144b2–179a4: 150a (*Complete Catalog of the Tibetan Buddhist Canons*, no. 136).

84 **The nature of birth is no birth:** *White Lotus of Compassion Scripture, Snying rje chen po'i pad ma dkar po zhes bya ba theg pa chen po'i mdo.* Sde dge Bka' 'gyur, Mdo sde, vol. Cha, fol. 56a1–128b7: 74a (*Complete Catalog of the Tibetan Buddhist Canons*, no. 111).

88 **"Rahula, my son":** *Scripture on the Concentrations of the Four Youths*, fol. 171a.

90 ***Scripture of the Great Passage from Suffering:*** *Yongs su mya ngan las 'das pa chen po'i mdo.* Sde dge Bka' 'gyur, Mdo sde, vol. Nya, fol. 1b1–ta 339a7 (*Complete Catalog of the Tibetan Buddhist Canons*, no. 119). Butön, *History of Buddhism*, vol. 2, p. 71.

91 **Master Shilapalita:** Tshul khrims bskyangs, *Lung phran tshegs kyi rnam par bshad pa.* Sde dge Bka' 'gyur, 'Dul ba, vol. Dzu, fol. 1b1–232a5.

91 **the great scholar Shakyashri:** Butön, *History of Buddhism*, vol. 2, p. 71.

91 ***Ornament for Scriptures:*** *Theg pa chen po mdo sde'i rgyan gyi tshig le'ur byas pa.* Sde dge Bka' 'gyur, Sems tsam, vol. Phi, fol. 1a1–39a4 (*Complete Catalog of the Tibetan Buddhist Canons*, no. 4020). L. Jampsal et al., translators, *The Universal Vehicle Discourse Literature.* New York: American Institute of Buddhist Studies, 2004, p. 80. Butön, *History of Buddhism*, vol. 2, p. 69.

91 ***Scripture on the Contemplation of Heroic Progress:*** *Dpa' bar 'gro ba'i ting nge 'dzin ces bya ba theg pa chen po'i mdo.* Sde dge Bka' 'gyur, Mdo sde, vol. Da, 253b5–316b6 (*Complete Catalog of the Tibetan Buddhist Canons*, no. 132). Etienne Lamotte, translator, *Suramgamasa-madhi*

Sutra: The Concentration of Heroic Progress; An Early Mahayana Buddhist Scripture, translated by Sara Boin-Webb. London: Curzon Press, 1998, p. 236. Butön, *History of Buddhism,* vol. 2, p. 69.

91 **Minor Monastic Precepts:** *'Dul ba phran tshegs gyi gzhi.* Sde dge Bka' 'gyur, 'Dul ba, vol. Tha-Da: vol. Da, fol. 246b.7 (*Complete Catalog of the Tibetan Buddhist Canons,* no. 6). Butön, *History of Buddhism,* vol. 2, p. 70.

91 **Explanation in Detail:** *Mahāvibhāṣā.* This work was not translated into Tibetan, though fragments such as this circulated within other texts. Butön, *History of Buddhism,* vol. 2, p. 70.

92 **Through the force of compassion:** This verse does not appear in Nagarjuna's *Precious Garland,* even though it is also said to be in Butön, *History of Buddhism,* vol. 1, p. 133.

92 **Scripture on the Buddha's Skill:** This passage does not appear in the *Thabs mkhas pa zhes bya ba theg pa chen po'i mdo.* Sde dge Bka' 'gyur, Mdo sde, vol. Za, fol. 283b2–310a7 (*Complete Catalog of the Tibetan Buddhist Canons,* no. 261), even though it is said to be according to Butön, *History of Buddhism,* vol. 1, p. 134.

EPILOGUE

97 **Epilogue:** Tibetan text: pp. 347.5–349.3.

97 **Living Out of the Game Scripture:** Bays, *The Voice of the Buddha.*

97 **White Lotus of Compassion Scripture:** White Lotus of Compassion Scripture, *Snying rje chen po'i pad ma dkar po zhes bya ba theg pa chen po'i mdo.* Sde dge Bka' 'gyur, Mdo sde, vol. Cha, fol. 56a1–128b7: 74a (*Complete Catalog of the Tibetan Buddhist Canons,* no. 111).

97 **Great Final Nirvana Scripture:** *Yongs su mya ngan las 'das pa chen po'i mdo.* Sde dge Bka' 'gyur, Mdo sde, vol. Nya, fol. fol. 1b1–ta 339a7 (*Complete Catalog of the Tibetan Buddhist Canons,* no. 119).

THE STORY OF RAHULA,
THE BUDDHA'S SON

99 **The Story of Rahula, the Buddha's Son:** Tibetan text: Bstan 'dzin chos rgyal, *'Phags pa'i gnas brtan chen po bcu drug gi rnam par thar pa rdzogs ldan sbyin pa'i rnga dbyangs,* in *Masterpieces of Bhutanese Biographical Literature.* New Delhi, 1970, pp. 351–429: pp. 358.4–363.

102 **It is certain, Rahula:** *'Phags pa khye'u bzhi'i ting nge 'dzin ces bya ba theg pa chen po'i mdo.* Sde dge Bka' 'gyur, Mdo sde, vol. Na, fol. 144b2–179a4: 171a (*Complete Catalog of the Tibetan Buddhist Canons,* no. 136).

NAGARJUNA'S "PRAISE TO
THE TWELVE ACTS"

103 **Nagarjuna's "Praise to the Twelve Acts":** Tibetan text: *Mdzad pa bcu gnyis kyi tshul la bstod pa.* Sde dge Bstan 'gyur, Bstod tshogs, vol. Ka, fols. 82b.3–83a.6 (*Complete Catalog of the Tibetan Buddhist Canons,* no. 1135).